MW00653309

STILL DANCING

One Dream, One Dog, One Stage

Ridding the World of Bullies
One School at a Time

GABRIELLE FORD

WITH DONNA RHINE

"NO SCHOOL BULLYING!"
Gabe and Izzy Publishing

Published by:
Gabe and Izzy Publishing
P.O. Box 1003
Fenton, MI 48430
www.gabeandizzy.com

Book jacket design by Christopher Tobias
Tobias' Outerwear for Books
www.tobiasdesign.com/

Book jacket photo © 2008 Joe Vaughn
Vaughn Media, Inc.
www.joevaughn.com

Author: Gabrielle Ford
Cover Design: Christopher Tobias
Editorial Team: Lynn DeGrande, Lisa Taylor, Alice Hagemeyer, Linda Lacina

Publisher's Cataloging-in-Publication Data

Ford, Gabrielle.
   Still Dancing: One dream, One Dog, One Stage. Ridding the World of Bullies One School at a
     Time / Gabrielle Ford; with Donna Rhine
        p. cm.
    ISBN-13-978-0-9841762-0-5
1. Friedreich's ataxia—Patients—Biography. 2. Adjustments (Psychology). 3.Women—Biography. I.
Title. II. Rhine, Donna, 1958–

                                     2009921468

Summary: Gabrielle Nicole Ford dreamed of becoming a prima ballerina, but those dreams were shattered. Diagnosed with a rare genetic neuro-muscular disease, Friedreich's ataxia, at the age of 12, Gabe not only struggled with the devastation of the illness, but endured constant and cruel bullying from classmates. Life changed dramatically for Gabe when Izzy, a beautiful and loving coonhound, came into her life. Izzy became Gabe's best friend and constant companion, and mysteriously developed a muscle disease with symptoms mirroring Gabe's.

For current information about releases by Gabrielle Ford visit www.gabeandizzy.com
Printed in the United States of America

In dedication:

To my mom and to my coonhound Izzy
for helping me to dance again.

Contents

Foreword

Nine and a half years ago when Gabe Ford walked into my office with her mother, her siblings and a puppy in tow, I naturally focused on the puppy. Who wouldn't when presented with an adorable coonhound with some of the largest ears God has ever created? Little did I know, Gabe was the real story, and through the next nine and a half years I would be impressed again and again with the strength and character of this young woman and the remarkable experience in which she had somehow chosen to include me.

The puppy was named Izzy and sadly, as it turned out, Izzy had some health issues. In life's quirky way, these health issues proved to be a Godsend as they propelled Gabe in directions I don't think she ever considered, and provided all of us with some of the most precious and profound experiences of our lives! Certainly for me, a veterinarian of 23 years, I have had many opportunities to meet extraordinary people and pets, but none with the impact of Gabe and Izzy.

The challenges they faced together, the growth I was able to watch, the very tiny part I was able to have in that growth all had a very positive and profound impact on my life. Gabe is truly an amazing woman, and I have been very privileged to have her touch my life. The following story is a testament to

Gabe, her spirit, and the bond between a young girl (soon to be woman) and a goofy coonhound with great big ears. I am richer for this story. I hope you are too.

Sincerely,
Dr. Sandy Smith
Izzy's veterinarian

CHAPTER ONE

Losing Balance

I was a dancer.

At the Lorraine Peltonen School of Dance, I steadied myself at the barre as I perfected my body's movements at the studio's wall-sized mirrors. I'd correct the angle of my pointed toe and pull my shoulders into the perfect dancer's posture. I wore a pink ribbon necklace with a pair of tiny pink ballet shoes around my neck. It was a reminder to others that dancing was the thing closest to my heart.

I was a dancer.

I wanted to learn everything I could. I was sure dancing was my destiny. I watched professional dancers onstage and on television and studied their movements. I even watched old Esther Williams movies from the fifties, with teams of swimmers dancing ballets underwater. Outside my bedroom, at home in Fenton, Michigan, was a closet with double sliding mirrored doors. Those mirrors became part of my personal dancer's studio. For seven years, I practiced and practiced in front of those closet doors, dreaming of performing those moves onstage.

By the time I was twelve, I'd danced tap, ballet and jazz. Many performances meant extra rehearsals and late nights. I didn't mind—it only meant I got to dance even more. Hours of practice left my legs aching and my feet sore. But I had never been happier. I was a dancer.

Those days, I thought I was honing my grace and my timing, but I was really perfecting my balance. Balance is key to holding poses and completing the simultaneous movements that comprise so many steps and positions. In one of my favorite poses, the arabesque, the dancer keeps one leg stretched and out to the back with the upper body straight and lifted, and one arm extended. In another beloved move, the pirouette, I'd spin 360 degrees on my tippy-toes. I would spin and spin, feeling the air rush by my ears, and wisps of hair break free from my tightly-crafted bun. I loved every minute of it.

I didn't realize then how easily balance had come to me—or how much I'd fight to keep it.

When I was twelve, I went with my family to my Uncle Steve and my Aunt Joanne's wedding. It was one of those perfect May weddings on a sunny afternoon. We were surrounded by red and white roses and loved ones ready to celebrate.

That sunny mood clouded when my grandfather, Papa, approached Mom at the reception. He wore a grim expression that set her on edge.

"Rhonda Kay," he said, "I'm concerned about Gabe. I can't be sure, but I think she might have gotten into the spiked punch bowl."

Mom laughed. "I don't think so, Dad." Could he have been joking?

But he wouldn't let it drop. "Well, something isn't right, Rhonda. She's not acting normal. Her balance is off."

"She wouldn't do anything like that," she said. Mom knew I'd just completed D.A.R.E., a drug prevention program at school and that I was adamantly against alcohol.

Papa wasn't convinced.

"Dad, there's just no way. Gabrielle wouldn't do anything like that."

Mom put it out of her mind and continued to enjoy the festivities. She didn't think anything more about it. I was fine. She was sure of it.

A few months later she received a surprise phone call—from my estranged father, Dennis. He didn't say "Hi" or "How are you?" Only, "Rhonda, I would like to see Gabe."

Mom was stunned to hear his voice on the line. "It's been years, Dennis. Why do you want to see Gabe now?"

"Well, it's about time. Don't you think?"

He had visitation rights but rarely used them. One time, when I was three, he was supposed to pick me up for the weekend. I waited by the front window all day with my little suitcase packed waiting for my father who never came. Memories like this had made her cautious and protective. "Can I ask you a question, Dennis?"

"Okay?"

"Do you have a dog?"

Confused, he said, "Yes, I have two. Why do you ask?"

"Do you love them?"

"Yes."

"Do you let them out of their cages and feed them every day?"

"Yes. What are you getting at, Rhonda?"

"My daughter should be treated better than a dog. You're welcome to come back into her life, but please don't walk out on her again and leave her in a cage wondering why her father has abandoned her for another twelve years.

An uncomfortable silence hung on the line before Mom said, "I'll talk to Gabe and see if she wants to see you. If she does, we'll set up a meeting."

Meeting my father after so much time was very awkward. "*Who was this person?*" I wondered. "*What am I even supposed to call him?*" Nothing about him was familiar. I hadn't seen him in years. He was a stranger.

Later, I agreed to go home with him for a visit. After all, weren't we family? Shouldn't this work in some strange, wonderful way?

But the home visit was even more awkward. I felt alone in a stranger's house. No one spent much time with me. I was on my own. I couldn't relax. I was even afraid to open the refrigerator to get something to eat or drink. It didn't feel like home.

During the visit, Dennis and his wife Tammy took me to the mall. They wanted to buy me things—things they thought I should want. Like different clothes and makeup. I was very uncomfortable. I knew how my mom felt about makeup.

It seemed like they wanted to transform me. They took me to a salon and had my long blond hair cut short, to the chin. I looked like a boy. I didn't even recognize myself in the mirror.

Tammy made sure I knew that I was not to expect this kind of treatment every time I visited. That was more than fine with me. I didn't expect or want anything from them. To be honest, I didn't want to go back.

Tammy pressured me to call Dennis "Dad." How could I? "Dad" was an endearing term for a man who loved and wanted to spend time with his child. Dennis had never been a "dad" to me, so mostly I referred to him as Dennis.

After the visit, Dennis took me home and sat with my mom at the kitchen table. It was a bizarre scene. There she sat with her ex-husband in her home with a daughter who was almost unrecognizable after only two days away. She was at a loss for words.

Dennis wasn't. He'd wanted to see me not to build our relationship, but to check out some rumors he'd heard about my health from other relatives.

When I went upstairs to my room he shared his concerns. He and Tammy had noticed that I had trouble squeezing the toothpaste out of the tube. And his brother Clayton, my uncle, thought there were neurological issues. As Dennis was responsible for my healthcare, he was determined to find out how my condition would impact him financially. Dennis wanted to take me to a doctor in the Flint area, about 20 minutes away. His brother was taking his son there and Dennis wanted me to be tested.

Mom was in shock. This man, this absentee father, thought he had a voice in my health care after just one weekend visit? Mom quickly told him, "We have a family doctor, Dennis. We love Dr. Daros. I have the utmost confidence in him. And besides, Gabe is at ease with him. There is no reason we can't just go to our doctor."

Dennis insisted, "I want Gabrielle to go to my brother's doctor."

Mom couldn't believe his nerve. She was overwhelmed. She didn't want anything from my father—even his advice. But he was my father and I was on his insurance plan. He had a voice. Being a peacekeeper by nature, Mom laid her uneasiness aside and let him have his way.

Dennis informed her that he would set up my appointment. When he called to tell Mom the appointment time, he asked, "Rhonda, do you know what muscular dystrophy is?"

"Yes." She had watched the Jerry Lewis MDA Telethons for many years. Her heart had always filled with compassion for these children, but she thought they were diagnosed with the disease at birth or shortly thereafter. Mom wondered why Dennis would mention this.

"I suspect that Gabe has some type of MD."

Her heart momentarily stopped. She thought, *"This just couldn't be."*

Dennis came with Mom and me to my first doctor's appointment, and while it was strange to have him around, we were not surprised when he just took over. He explained that both his brother and he had noticed my balance and coordination seemed abnormal. The doctor checked my reflexes and ordered a CAT scan, along with several other tests. After all of the results came back, the office called and asked Dennis, Mom, and me to come in for a consultation.

Mom was concerned. She assumed there must be something wrong if we were being called in for a "consultation." To Mom's surprise, the doctor told us my tests were all normal. He recommended some form of exercise program to further develop my coordination. Mom politely agreed, but inside she was confused. I *was* coordinated. For the past seven years, I ate and breathed ballet, tap, and jazz.

We were thankful for the good report but couldn't call the day a success. When Dennis took us home he informed us of all the ways he'd parent me differently. He implied that perhaps my voice trembled at times because Mom was too strict. He said he thought I was more immature than most twelve-year-old girls. He believed I should be wearing make-up and doing a whole lot of other things differently. No doubt, his parenting ideas were different than Mom's, but those differences did not make her a bad parent. Mom tried not to take his words to heart. She was relieved when he finally left that day.

Her relief didn't last long. A week later, a call came from the doctor. I remember the call like it was yesterday:

"I'm really sorry," said the voice on the other line, "but there has been a terrible mistake. Our office staff mixed up Gabrielle's test results with another patient who has the same last name." I later found out that the other patient was my cousin who was being tested for headaches.

Mom was in shock. Knowing I was in the other room, she did her best to keep her composure, but it wasn't easy. What the doctor revealed halted the blood flow to her veins.

"I'm really sorry to have to tell you this, but all of Gabe's test results came out abnormal. Her cerebellum is atrophying."

Mom could not believe a physician would give her this kind of a diagnosis over the phone. How cruel! In truth, she felt like she was going to pass out. "I'm going to get you an appointment with a pediatric neurologist at the University of Michigan, Mott Children's Hospital. We'll call you back and let you know when her appointment is."

Mom didn't tell me anything that day. She just couldn't.

Three months passed before U of M could get me in. The day Mom and I went to the doctor's office is a blur. I knew I was going for added testing and that Dennis was going to meet us there, but I didn't understand what all the fuss was about. In my mind, I was a perfectly normal twelve-year-old girl.

The doctor examined my spine while Mom asked questions. She didn't want to upset me, so she was careful not to ask too much.

"Do you suspect she has some type of progressive condition?"

The physician nodded. "Yes, I do." Upon finishing his exam, the doctor sent me immediately for an electromyogram (EMG).

The nurse who came to get me was sweet and caring, putting Mom somewhat at ease. When the nurse wrapped her arm around my shoulder, I gladly walked with her down a long hallway.

Mom, suddenly all too aware of what these tests could confirm, watched me walk away. As she did, she noticed for the first time the subtle changes that everyone else had seen. My gait was slightly different, wobbly even. The realization hit her hard and fast. There really was something wrong with me, her beautiful daughter.

As much as it tore at her heart, she could not look away until I disappeared around a corner.

Alone with Dennis in the doctor's office, mom's eyes filled with tears. The doctor suspected that I had a disease of the central nervous system called Friedreich's ataxia (FA). Degeneration of the nerve tissue in the spinal cord creates unsteadiness, speech problems and even heart disease. Usually, within 10–15 years after symptoms appear, the patient is confined to a wheelchair.

Others can become incapacitated. The doctor believed a test would confirm his suspicions. If I had FA, I would be only the second case this doctor had ever diagnosed. The other case was a boy, and he died when he was twenty-one. Mom was devastated.

Dennis had no patience for crying. He gave mom one of his stone-cold looks and pointed his index finger at her face. His frigid words sent chills up her spine. "You're going to have to be strong, Rhonda!"

Deep inside she knew he was right, but his lack of warmth tore at her heart. She didn't understand his coldness. I was his daughter, too. Mom knew exactly what he was really saying. This was her problem, not his, and she was the one who'd need to buck up and deal with it.

Mom tried to hold herself together, but she could not stem the flow of tears. Suddenly, she needed to talk to someone who cared about her and me. She left the office for a short while and called my grandparents.

Mom walked away from the office that day knowing full well just how rare this disease the doctor suspected I had was. But she still could not bring herself to tell me their suspicions. The holidays approached and she had no desire to spoil them for me. When the findings did come in and confirmed I had FA, mom still stayed silent. Christmas came and went, and I thought I was just another normal twelve year old. Mom trimmed the house for the holidays and went through the motions of our family traditions keeping the secret to herself. I have since learned that she cried herself to sleep trying to find the courage to tell me that I would never dance again.

I saw my father only a few times after my diagnosis. Mom wanted me to develop a relationship with my father, thinking it would make me whole. I tried, but he wouldn't meet with me regularly. He'd only meet at his convenience. I wasn't convinced he wanted to be a part of my life.

One day when he drove me back home to Fenton, he told Mom, "She's too quiet. I told her that she had to talk to me on the way home. If she didn't, I wasn't coming to get her anymore."

Mom was stunned. "Give her a chance, Dennis. Gabe has forgiven you for all the years you neglected her, but she needs time to open up with you." He came back to our home one other time—two Christmases after Mom and Dennis learned my diagnosis.

Mom had gone out of her way to buy a gift for me to give Dennis and Tammy. She even left the house so the three of us could spend some time alone. I shouldn't have been surprised when he pulled into the driveway, came in alone, handed me a gift, and said, "We're on our way to the airport. We're spending the holiday in the Bahamas."

I haven't seen Dennis since. I am not angry with him. I can't be. After all the years without him there simply isn't a desire to create a bond, a bond has never been there.

Six months after my diagnosis—and two days after my thirteenth birthday—my parents, along with Aunt Joanne, sat down with me at our kitchen table and told me about my disease. Uncle Steve was there, but he was so broken inside he left the room just before they told me the news.

I cried. "Am I going to have to quit dancing?" It was the first question I asked.

Mom hated to tell me, but hiding the truth would not help me come to terms with my future. "Yes, Gabe. This is already affecting the way you walk."

I had to know. "Am I going to have to spend the rest of my life in a wheelchair?"

Mom was in tears when she admitted, "One day, Gabe."

The news was more than I could bear. My tears dried up and I refused to discuss it further. I made my way to my bedroom and closed the door.

The next day, I refused to go to school. At a loss for how to handle this, Mom asked a school counselor to come to the house. The woman promised that our conversation would be confidential. She lied.

As if coming to terms with my disease was not enough, when I returned to school the following day, it was more than apparent the counselor had been talking. I don't think she did so maliciously, but a classmate came up to me that morning and asked, "Do you have AIDS, Gabe?"

I was angry. Although deep down I knew how she found out I was ill, I asked her anyway. "Why would you say that?"

The girl admitted, "The counselor told me you have a disease." I felt betrayed.

From then on, I never confided in a teacher or a counselor again. In truth, I didn't want to talk to anyone about my disease. I was still in denial. To talk about it would make it real, and I didn't want it to be real. Who would?

I was thirteen and my diagnosis made me feel very scared and alone. While I didn't know it then, FA only stole my muscular control. FA didn't steal my ability to connect to people. It didn't steal my ability to trust others or reach out to them. It didn't even steal my ability to connect with people on stage. I was still a dancer. In fact, Gabrielle Nicole Ford, would dance again, and for thousands. It's just that I would dance in a way I'd never dreamed possible.

CHAPTER TWO

Bullied

A few weeks after learning about my diagnosis, I sat near a table while Mom stood and brushed my long blonde hair. "Gabe," Mom said, "I've been thinking about your illness and how it has been impacting you."

I could tell this was going to be another "Mom talk." But since I really liked the way she brushed my hair, I stayed and listened. "We know that eventually you won't be able to walk, honey, but I want us to take this one day at a time. We aren't going to keep looking back. We've got to go forward and make every day count. We need to approach each new day as the best day we have."

"That's fine with me, Mom," I responded, "but I need everyone to do something for me. I don't want anyone to keep mentioning words that are associated with my disease. I can't dwell on it. If I do, I'll get depressed. I would rather deal with the realities of my condition as they unfold."

Mom knew exactly what I was implying. Not even words like "wheelchair," "Friedreich's ataxia," "walker," "cane," "leg braces," or "neuro-muscular dis-ease" were to be mentioned in the house. I went so far as to ask my family not to watch the Jerry Lewis telethons while I was around. They frightened me. I couldn't handle seeing others suffer, knowing I would be just like them one day.

Mom, always the protector, wanted me to know I wasn't the only one out there with Friedreich's ataxia. She called the MDA, and they gave her the names of several other teens with the disease. After a few arranged meetings, I told Mom I didn't want to hang around them. I didn't think I was better than any of the kids I met, but they constantly wanted to talk about their disease; I didn't. I could appreciate Mom's good intentions, but talking about my disease wasn't helping me to move forward. Talking about my disease only made me depressed.

A new school year was starting. I would begin the eighth grade and since my school spanned the eighth through twelfth grades, I would start high school. Like my friends, I looked forward to my teen years. Dating, driving and school dances were all at the forefront of my mind.

Still, I felt insecure and out of place. This would be my first year in a new district, with new faces. It would also be the first year I'd start school diagnosed with Friedreich's ataxia. I had convinced myself that no one would want to be my friend if they knew about my disease. Why would they like someone who was so different?

I made it my personal goal to make it through high school and my graduation ceremony without using any adaptive equipment. Although a few close friends knew about my disease, I did my best to hide it. I had convinced myself that others saw me as normal, when in fact they did not. Even before I was diagnosed, others could see that the way I walked was different. I never realized that there was anything wrong with me. Many thought I was stupid. Although my grades did suffer, it was not because I was incapable of doing the schoolwork. It was because it took all of my effort to concentrate on my every move. Above all, I was determined to look normal—or at least what I perceived as normal.

In truth, I was so determined to appear normal and fit in with the crowd, I put my disease out of my mind. To me, that meant it didn't exist. This made me a target for bullies.

At first some kids made snide comments about my slurred speech and wobbly gait, but I assumed they were just making fun of me because I was new to the school. However, when the snide comments and outright bullying persisted over several months, I began to wonder if they were on to me—that they knew my deep dark secret. What else could it be?

My horrible experiences in choir class made me wonder if others were on to me as well. A group of popular girls would pick apart my appearance. One girl in particular would remind me that I needed to get my split ends cut off, and then another girl would criticize my clothes. She said I wasn't cool because I didn't wear designer jeans. When I finally found a pair on the clearance rack, I was excited about being able to show them off, but when I got to school, the girl only laughed at me. The jeans Mom bought were the right brand, but she told me they were for boys! Regardless, whether they were or not, I never wore them again. Mom kept asking me why I didn't wear the jeans I had begged her for, but how could I tell her kids made fun of me for wearing boy's jeans?

As if the constant heckling about my clothes and hair were not enough, all through choir that same mean girl sat behind me and hit me on the head with her thick music book. I was sick of her constant abuse. Out of desperation, I mentioned it to Mom, and it turned out that she had gone to school with the girl's mom. Mom decided to call her. She and Mom talked on and on like it was old times. The woman was embarrassed by her daughter's behavior and said she'd talk to her. Soon after the phone call, the girl apologized to me at school. In truth, I was just glad to have the torment come to an end—with her, anyway. While I didn't appreciate it at the time, I'd just learned the most important lesson about fighting bullies: speaking up is the first step to finding a solution. Unfortunately, I couldn't see that then. Looking back, in those early days, I was definitely in denial. I still saw myself as the healthy and active dancer I had been not so very long ago. I was ashamed of my disease and how it impacted me, but I was too embarrassed to admit I needed help. I was just one girl surrounded by crowds of bullies. How could I make things change?

While all forms of bullying can leave deep scars, the name-calling plagued me the most. A favorite for bullies was to call me "drunk." Classmates often walked by me and hurled their comments.

"Are you drunk?"

"You're walking like you're drunk."

"You talk like you're drunk! You really ought to lay off the booze, Gabe!"

Of course I wasn't drunk, but this is how many perceived the way my illness changed me. I was still in denial and trying to hide my symptoms, so I wasn't about to confide in my classmates. The way they treated me now was bad enough.

Like many teens, I had a problem with acne. One student, whose complexion was just as bad as mine, referred to me as "pizza face." Since he was in the popular crowd, others thought it was funny and chimed in.

I lived close enough to walk home from high school. It was a half-mile walk, but along a busy road without sidewalks. The shoulder was really a long ditch that was bumpy and gravelly. I needed to concentrate very hard to walk on this road. During these walks some of my classmates would either follow me or walk on the opposite side of the street. One girl would initiate derogatory comments. She seemed to acquire the greatest pleasure when she called me a "slut." I'm clueless as to why she chose this particular name when nothing could have been further from the truth, but that didn't seem to matter to her. She also told people I had a brain tumor. Her friends would come up to me and ask, "What's wrong with you, Gabe? Got a brain tumor?"

As if hurling their insults at me weren't enough, my family became a target as well. I will never forget the day my little sister Caitlin ran off the school bus crying hysterically. The kids on the bus were making fun of me and told her we were "trailer trash" because we lived in a modular home park. Caitlin was only seven years old at the time.

Intimidation was a daily fact of my high school life. One day in the gym two popular girls came up to me as I sat on the bleachers. One stood in front of me and threatened, "My friend likes the boy you've been talking to. If you don't stop talking to him, I'm going to slap you." Then, to add insult to the threat, the other one told me I was ugly. I was confused. The boy and I were just friends. He sat behind me in one of my classes. Still, the girls managed to intimidate me and I did my best to steer clear of that boy.

Another day, in biology class, two other girls hovered over me. Another girl had told them that I told the teacher that they copied off her homework. They threatened to beat me up. I had no idea what they were talking about and tried to set them straight. They wouldn't listen to the truth. Knowing that these girls had a reputation of beating up other girls, I took their threats seriously.

While many would justify these kinds of behaviors as boys being boys, or girls being girls, their actions were blatantly wrong. They were not justifiable.

I kept silent about the bullying. I wanted Mom to think the kids at my new school liked me. I didn't want to worry her. Besides, I was embarrassed. How could I tell her that I felt that some of my new classmates found pleasure in tormenting me?

In addition, I couldn't see beyond my pain and frustration. I had lost my trust in school counselors when I was first diagnosed, and now I honestly believed that no one really cared. Even if I were to tell any of the school staff, I didn't think anything would change. I convinced myself that no one would take me seriously, so I held everything inside.

I withdrew so much, I started to avoid groups of kids whenever I could. The bullying turned every high school event—especially pep rallies—into a potential landmine. Because the cheerleaders and jocks were in charge of these events, there were no guarantees I would not be called down and made a spectacle of in front of the whole school. I did my best to skip these assemblies, but there were times when it was impossible. From the moment

I'd enter the gym and take a seat on the bleachers, the inner turmoil would begin. Although these simple games were fun for some, for me, they were very difficult. I would breathe a huge sigh of relief when a pep rally ended and a game finally began without me being singled out. For that day, at least, I had been overlooked.

Bathrooms were popular spots for girls to hang out, so I avoided them as much as I could. Even walking by them made me nervous. Fear of confrontation caused me to steer clear. I also avoided the cafeteria. I often ate my lunch in a classroom instead, with a teacher nearby. I felt safer that way.

The verbal torments often escalated into physical abuse. In high school, I dreaded walking to and from my classes in the eighth grade hall. Lake Fenton High School was housed in an old building with sloping, inclined floors. I struggled to balance on them, always afraid I might fall. The stampede of students moving though that narrow hall made the passage even more difficult. Some shoved me on purpose just to watch me stumble. Other students pushed me into students just to embarrass me. They were cruel. I took more bullying than anyone knew. After all, who could I tell?

Walking the senior hallway was a nightmare. Classmates knocked my books out of my hands and kicked them down the hall. Many students thought it was funny to play foot hockey with my books and watch me scramble after them.

It was nothing for someone to walk by my locker and slam it shut just after I had gotten it open. One day, the boy in the next locker reached over my head to grab the CDs I kept on the top shelf of my locker. He waved them in front of me, taunting and teasing me. Then, he walked away with them. He never did give them back.

Other kids threw things at me—everything from spit wads, eraser tips, paperclips and pencils to pieces of chewed-up plastic and chalk. Pieces would hit my face and get lodged in my hair. Even when the missiles simply landed on my desk, it was still degrading.

One particular boy got some sort of perverse thrill out of punching me with his fist on my outer thigh. Because he was in most of my classes and his locker was close to mine, avoidance was next to impossible. If he sat in front of me, he'd turn around and annoy me by making fun of the way my mouth moved when I talked. Once he started, the other students joined in, mocking the way my jaw moved back and forth to taunt me. They also mimicked the way I walked.

One day, Mom noticed the bruises on my leg. She insisted on knowing where I had gotten them. I didn't want to tell her, so I slipped into my bedroom, trying to avoid her. She was right on my heels, and she wanted the truth. She was very upset when I finally told her.

Mom went straight to the phone and called the assistant principal. We were both shocked when he didn't seem like he wanted to be involved. He asked her what she wanted him to do about the situation.

Mom responded, "You're the assistant principal, I was thinking you would tell me." When he still offered no solutions, Mom said, "I would like this young man called to the office and spoken to, and I also think he should apologize to Gabe and promise he'll stop his behavior."

Though he agreed and said he'd get back to her with a phone call, he never did. Mom went above the assistant principal's head, calling the principal himself. Principal Jerry Kramer took immediate action. He asked the assistant principal to apologize for not handling the problem more swiftly. He also called me and the young man to the school office, talking to each of us separately. The boy apologized to me that day, and I was pleasantly surprised by the change in him. He was actually nice to me after that. I learned again the importance of coming forward. Bullies can change their behavior and speaking up can resolve conflicts.

The issue was even instructive to others. Years later, Mom ran into a teacher from my old high school and she told her this story. The other woman hadn't experienced bullying at the school and dismissed the possibility. "Maybe this boy liked Gabe!" Mom was appalled. Physical and verbal abuse is not a compliment. Mom explained to her how prevalent bullying had been at the school and how it impacted me. The conversation eventually made that teacher more sensitive to bullying. She later told Mom that she had learned that bullying was a serious issue, and that she now tries to correct it in her classroom. Mom and I have a great deal of respect for those who are willing to stand up and do what is right instead of ignoring bullying and hoping it will go away.

I looked for my happiness outside of school. In many ways I found it through my after-school jobs. Mom had a rule that all her kids had to hold a job when we were of age. She didn't treat me any differently than my other siblings.

My school offered a summer job program for special needs kids the summer after my freshman year. They asked me to work as a secretary for a couple of hours each morning in the bus garage. In the afternoons, I would work as a janitor. I had mixed feelings—at first I thought they wanted to hire me out of pity because they thought I couldn't find a job anywhere else. Mom pushed me into it, though, and I was glad she did. She knew it would be good for me. My duties at the bus garage were small, but they gave me pride. As a secretary, I answered phones, made copies and filed. As a janitor, I washed classroom and hallway floors, changed light bulbs and cleaned blackboards.

At work, no one called me names. People treated me as an equal. I was proud to contribute and to be trusted with important tasks.

In my eleventh and twelfth grade years, I worked at Farmer Jack, a grocery store. In so many ways, this was a positive experience for me. I loved knowing others depended on my help.

The winter before graduation, on the night of a horrible ice and snow-storm, my mom came to pick me up from work. She had made it clear to me that I could bag groceries, but I was not allowed to go out into the parking lot to gather up grocery carts during the winter.

When she pulled into the parking lot, there I was with my blue Adidas jacket doing my best to gather carts with the snow blowing in my face. My eyelashes were thick with snowflakes—as if I were wearing white mascara—but I happily attended to my job.

Mom did not share my sentiments. "Gabe!" she bellowed out, "What are you doing?"

I looked at her, my hood covering half my forehead, my red face full of snow and said, "Let me do this while I still can, Mom!"

She understood that I was trying to do more than just my job. She jumped out of the car and said, "Let me help you!"

Together we gathered all of the carts, laughing, as they slipped and slid in the heavy snow. We shoved the now wet carts toward Farmer Jack's doors, and they hit the automatic adjacent doormats and rolled back outside! Mom and I laughed till we were sure we couldn't laugh anymore.

Senior year, prom approached and my classmates buzzed about who was going with whom. In art class, cliques would congregate at different tables. At one table was a bunch of hockey players. One of the students in that clique had a foreign exchange student living at his house. They told me the exchange student did not have a date, so the kids in that group asked me if I would ask him to go to the prom. It took me a few days to get up the nerve to ask him, but I finally did. He was in the lunchroom when I went up to him and asked. It was obvious that the kids knew he would say no; they were just doing this to embarrass me. When the guy turned me down, everyone laughed.

I did end up going to the prom with a good friend. Had it not been for this caring young man, I would not have gone. As it turned out, I had a really good time with Aaron. I wore a celery green floor-length dress with a high neck and lace across the bodice. I wore my hair piled into curls on top of my head. It was a great night and I'm glad I didn't let those bullies take it from me.

Despite my hardships, I had a select group of close friends. One of these friends was Amanda, who I met in the eighth grade. She was also new to school that year we met and we helped each other through it. At first she seemed loud to me, but I learned from her how wrong it is to trust assumptions. She's actually very sensitive and caring. She always accepted me. While my disease seemed to embarrass others, it never seemed to bother her at all. We'd spend a lot of time together, doing homework, instant messaging by computer, walking to the store for candy or pop and going out on her family's boat. It was a true friendship like this one that made the bullying bearable.

My graduation ceremony was scheduled to take place at Whiting Auditorium in Flint. Although I was excited about all the day would hold, my apprehensions escalated the minute I saw the steps leading up and down from the stage.

After calming down a bit, I took a closer look. I was sure that, if I concentrated, I could make it up and down the steps without making a fool of myself. Although I hoped I was right, uncertainty lingered in the hidden recesses of my mind.

My graduating class lined up in one of the outer hallways before we entered the auditorium. I moved along without a hitch—until I was halfway to my seat, when a downward step caught me unaware. My ankle twisted and I fell to the floor. I was mortified. I wanted to die. My Uncle Steve came running up the stairs to help me. As much as I appreciated his efforts and concern, I was afraid that his actions only drew more attention. I convinced myself that every eyeball in the building was on me. I wondered if my graduation would go down in history as the one that was ruined by Gabrielle Ford. I could only hope everyone would forget about my blunder before it was time to walk up front and receive my diploma.

I sat on pins and needles during the ceremony, dreading hearing my name called. My determination to walk across the stage and receive my diploma without using any adaptive equipment remained strong, despite the horrific pain in my ankle. When my name was finally called, I stood and moved toward the stairs. This was it. All I had to do was make it up the stairs, across the stage, and back down the stairs. This had been my personal goal since I was first diagnosed; I refused to give up when I was so close.

The second I accepted my diploma, relief washed over me. I had finally made it into the real world. As my class walked off the stage, we were each handed a gerbera daisy. The Beatles song *Here Comes the Sun* rang out as we exited the building. Inside, I jumped for joy. No doubt about it. A new day was dawning.

Though I graduated, the night wasn't quite over. A lock-in held at the high school called Project Graduation was planned following the ceremony. Its purpose was to help keep students safe on graduation night. My purpose was to enjoy it just like any other senior. My ankle was killing me from my fall, but I didn't let on. Not even Mom knew.

At the lock-in, the parent volunteers had transformed the school gym into an Amazon rainforest. With such a change, on such a night, everything seemed possible. And maybe anything was. The cliques that had divided our class throughout five years of high school seemed to disappear. I was worried classmates had heard about my fall and would make fun of me. Only one did, but fortunately, he was the only one. Mostly, my class spent the night celebrating each other and enjoying a real night to remember.

The gym was packed with activities with everything from sumo wrestling—where many classmates put on fat suits and wore wigs to help them look the part—to human foosball played inside a huge inflatable arena. Tricycle races, a poker room, dancing below a disco ball, and potato sack races were just some of the other amusements. We could even have our pictures taken behind Tarzan and Jane cut-outs for our scrapbooks.

I enjoyed myself but my ankle kept me from getting involved in the games. I mostly stood around and talked to friends. Toward the end of the night, I found myself looking for a place to sit.

The highlight of the night came at the raffle drawing. Many local merchants had donated prizes to be given away. I was leaning against the stage for balance when I heard my name called out. I was in shock. I'd never won anything before. My family and I were huge fans of the Red Wings, so winning Chris Osgood's jersey was a big deal to me.

Little did I know, my mom stood in the doorway of the gym. As she heard my name called, she threw her arm in the air and yelled, "Way to go Gabe! That's my girl!"

Mom hugged me tightly and joined me at the table with my friends. Even the boy who had been punching me in the leg at school was with us. It wasn't like we were the best of friends, but because of the way the principal had handled that awkward situation, healing had occurred. Mom even took our picture. It was good to put that hurt behind me.

"Mom," I asked, "why did you come to pick me up so early? I'm not ready to leave."

"I didn't plan to, Gabe, but I woke up out of a deep sleep around four o'clock this morning, threw on my jeans, and drove quickly to the school. I sensed that something was wrong. Instead, I had the amazing sight of watching you win Osgood's jersey. Some things are just meant to be."

Later that evening, after I had slept all day, I called Mom to my room and asked, "Will you take a look at my ankle?" As soon as she did, we were off to the emergency room. My ankle was half the size of a baseball.

I had a torn ligament, so they put me in an air cast, and after further examination, diagnosed me with mono.

As we headed home from the hospital that night, I could only contemplate what life after high school would be like. I would no longer have to pretend to hide my disease. Yes, I was still in denial, convincing myself that I had made it through school without many classmates knowing about my disease. I realize now that the way I perceived things was not always the way they were. In my heart and mind, I was finally free to be me for the first time in years.

CHAPTER THREE

Changes

My graduation money burned a hole in my pocket. I could hear the Genesee Valley Mall in Flint calling my name. After injuring my ankle at the Senior Party, I couldn't walk without support, so Mom became my walker. She took me to the mall to spend some of my graduation loot and walked arm in arm with me visiting store after store. I checked out all my favorites—Wilson's Leather, Hudson's and Lady Foot Locker, just to name a few. My bags swelled with goodies—including shirts, jeans, perfume and a heavy three-quarter-length leather coat.

We shopped till we dropped—literally. Though I'd rested periodically throughout the day, by the end, my right knee ached something fierce. As I left Hudson's on my way back to the car, my knee gave out; I slipped out of Mom's arm and fell to the ground.

This was the last day Mom and I were able to walk like this in a mall. I'd already needed to quit my job bagging groceries at Farmer Jack. I couldn't stand for hours on end like I used to. Eventually, standing for any period of time was unbearably painful and I could only walk if I held onto something—

the wall, a chair, or a counter top. Mom would go out on errands and I would go along for the ride, but I would always stay in the car. Someone else would always do the legwork.

Mom said it made her sad. She was afraid I was giving in to my disease. She was right to a degree. I was struggling, but I couldn't help it. Walking became more and more difficult, and I wasn't about to use a wheelchair. I refused to become dependent on anything.

While the changes from my disease were inevitable, I hadn't expected the other changes that graduation brought. Within a few months after graduation, my mom and stepdad Rick purchased the house Mom grew up in. There were not any kids my age living in the new neighborhood, so I wasn't thrilled with the move, but the choice was not mine to make. I made the best of it. For years I had focused solely on making it through high school, and looking as normal as possible. I was not emotionally ready to say good-bye to the few friends I had. Learning that most of them were not going away for college encouraged me. I thought that meant they would still want to be a part of my life. I needed friends around me. In truth, I was afraid of being alone. Determined to stay in touch, I called several of my friends; none of them returned my calls. It was as if they had all disappeared. One day I had friends and school to keep me busy, the next day there was nothing, and I was home alone. There was no transition.

So I stayed home, away from the eyes I was certain gawked at my awkward steps and slow speech. I hid, defending myself from the harsh words I was sure I'd hear. I couldn't bear the thought of running into bullies from school. Mom and Rick worked full time and my sisters were in school. Being home alone all day gave me time to think, maybe too much time. I just stayed home and slept a lot—too much! Often, Mom came home from work and found me curled up, sleeping on the living room floor—like a small animal.

In an attempt to fight depression, I'd take a shower as soon as I'd wake up in the morning. As soothing as the water was, I could only stay in there for so long. My life lacked meaning and purpose. Often, Mom found me with my head on the kitchen or picnic table. Sometimes I lay like that for hours. I barely existed.

Mom knew I was depressed, but she didn't know how to help me. I kept asking her why my friends wouldn't call.

She tried her best to console me. "After graduating from high school," she once told me, "it's normal for people to journey off into new endeavors. They find a new freedom they've never known before. It's not that they don't like you, Gabe, it's just that they are finally free."

This news only made me feel sadder. Did they think of me as excess baggage? I'd like to believe that if our roles were reversed, I would have been there for them.

"I just don't understand, Mom. Why can't their newfound freedom include me?"

Watching my body digress was unsettling—a reality check. In my mind, I was still dancing, walking, riding a bike and much more, but in truth, I couldn't do any of those activities any longer. It was as if I were an amputee. I was still so used to having a normal life that I didn't remember I didn't until I tried to live one. I became angry, frustrated, and often mean. Another night, I unloaded a day's worth of anguish on my mom the moment she came home from work.

"Look at me, Mom. I mean, really look at me! My body is changing so fast. I can't walk and get around like I used to. I'm ashamed of myself. Can you understand why I don't want people to see me this way? I'm so different."

It took Mom by surprise. She quickly told me, "It doesn't matter what other people think. You can't go on like this, Gabe. You're robbing yourself of the life you've been given. You need to go and live it. Remember what we talked about? You need to make every day count."

I could see that mom was fighting tears, so I forced myself to calm down, but I still had more to say. "I'm not mad or angry that I'm ill, Mom," I said.

"I'm just afraid of running into former classmates who used to make fun of me. If they made fun of me when I was walking, what will they think of me now?"

A friend invited me to a New Year's Eve party. While I was thrilled to be included, the thought of meeting new people was a bit scary.

This time, I was determined to push past my fears. I accepted the invitation.

When I started getting dressed for the occasion, my enthusiasm escalated. There was a certain boy who was going to be at this party, so I went out of my way to look my best.

I wasn't the only one in our family with plans for the evening. Mom was having a party, so she hustled around, making food and cleaning the house. The Christmas decorations were still up for the New Year's party—real garland and red bows on the porch with candles in each window. Mom set luminary bags into the snow to light the path to the door and set the table with snacks such as crudités and fresh dipping shrimps.

Although I wondered when my friend was planning to pick me up, he had never given me a specific time. I waited patiently in my bedroom. However, when mom's guests began arriving and still I hadn't heard from him, I got a little edgy. Was he actually going to come? Was I being stood up?

I had been so excited about this night—even day dreamed about what it would be like. After all, doesn't everybody want to be with people their own age on New Year's Eve? I loved my mom's friends, but I feared that everyone would know what had happened. How humiliating to be ditched on New Year's Eve.

As the minutes turned into hours, my hopeful heart plunged into despair. He was not coming, and the realization hit me hard. Disappointment turned into anger as I made my way into the living room. Mom looked at me with sympathy while my cheeks burned in embarrassment. "I know you're disappointed, Gabe, but you're welcome to join us."

I exploded. "Why would I want to do that, Mom?" The room grew quiet—too quiet. Everyone heard me, but I didn't care. Without another word, I scooted off to my room and spent the rest of the night alone.

My friend humiliated me and I humiliated my mom. Her friends had no idea how much I was struggling, or even what had happened to bring on my outburst. In her embarrassment, Mom didn't even try to explain my actions, leaving them in the dark.

She didn't tell me how she felt until the next day. She told me I needed to write letters to her friends, apologizing for my behavior. I didn't want to do it, but I knew I was in the wrong. I was hurt that my friend didn't come through for me, but I had no right to take it out on anyone else. Having been bullied most of my life, I knew the damage it could do, and I didn't want that. I wrote the letters.

In the midst of these dark times, there were those special few who went out of their way to reach out to me. For instance, one of our neighbors seemed to understand my loneliness, so around the holidays she would come to get me and we'd go off to her house to make cream cheese cookies together— incredibly delicious cream cheese cookies. Visiting with her was always a joy. It meant a lot to me to know that she would take time out of her busy schedule just for me. She always seemed to pull me up when I was down. And there was an added bonus to our visits: I'd always come home with a huge plate full of cookies to share with my family. We'd eat them for days.

When I think of the fun we had during those times, it saddens me to know there were others who tried to reach out to me and I'd refused to acknowledge them. I was so angry and hurt most of the time. I couldn't see what I was doing to those around me and myself.

I ruined many family events. I wasn't always so nice to be around. My bad attitude spoiled trips to the mall and family dinners at restaurants. I wouldn't cooperate and my family would be embarrassed or frustrated and even walk away from me.

One time I shredded my handicapped-parking sticker because I didn't want Mom parking in those spots when we'd go out together. When Mom found out, she told me if I did it again, I'd have to pay her fifty dollars for the time involved to replace it.

I became afraid Mom would give up on me. I should have known better, but fear was robbing me of all that I knew to be true. Although there were times when Mom was at the end of her rope, her unending love could weather the most ravaging storm.

My sisters were understanding and wonderful for the most part. But there were those times I'd push them too far. I remember Caitlin being fed up with me several times. I couldn't blame her. As much as I wanted to change, I didn't know how to move past my pain. I could be pure nastiness.

Was I beyond hope of ever living a normal life? All my family wanted was for me to be with them. Instead, I would hide away, too miserable to see what I was doing to all of them. It was so much easier to stay in my tight little world of despair, refusing to let others see the real Gabrielle Ford.

Mom was right: I had to start living the life I'd been given. I needed to make every day count.

Mom had always told me that I needed to have a goal to work toward after graduation. I had to go to school or hold a job. I developed a love for criminology and travel. After much consideration, I decided on The Travel Academy and enrolled in a local school in Flint. I'd always read brochures and books about foreign lands and watched the Travel Channel frequently.

As it turned out, one of the travel school instructors happened to be my former babysitter. Many years had slipped away since we last spoke, so we had a lot to talk about. Another instructor happened to be a former neighbor. This was good news, easing my apprehensions about starting at a new school and meeting new friends.

At the Academy, I studied geography, military time, airport codes, and how to book trips, car rentals, trains and cruises. The school introduced me to places I'd love to see first-hand, such as India, Greece and Thailand. In four months, I received my certificate.

Mom and Rick gave me rides to and from school, about a half-hour drive from our home. Once at the school, mom would wrap her arm around my waist to help me walk to class and into my seat. My balance was gone, so I would have fallen over if she hadn't been there to help. So many times, at the end of a school day, Mom returned, stooped down and said, "Get on my back, it's easier," and, off we'd go, back to the car.

The laughter we shared during these times was good for our souls. My arms would wrap around her neck, and she'd tell me not to choke her. Many times when I'd use her as a walker, we'd laugh and act like we were dancing when my legs would become too wobbly.

She knew me well. If it weren't for her, I would not have gone anywhere. Although some would say she was enabling me, keeping me from facing reality, I was just not ready emotionally to use a wheelchair. In my heart I knew, once I did, there was no turning back. Mom tried to persuade me to accept a wheelchair, or a walker, but I refused. I had not used a wheelchair yet, and I didn't plan on using one any time soon. Although she didn't want me in one if I didn't need to use one, she worried about my falls and visits to the emergency room.

When I told her I was going to do this my way, she let it go. The thought of my former classmates seeing me using a walker or wheelchair tortured me. If they made fun of me when I was still walking, what would they say or think if they saw me using adaptive equipment? I was a dancer who now needed a wheelchair. How could I give in to my disease? I was still feisty, still a fighter. I was determined to walk as long as I could.

Some people told mom that I needed to get over my aversion. That was easy for them to say when they weren't losing their independence—their ability to walk. They had no right to judge me. It wasn't as if I were sitting in judgment of others. Perhaps if they had to walk in my shoes for a day, they would have better understood my struggle. I was pretty sure they would want to walk forever, too.

I managed simple tasks. My family would offer to help, but my response was usually a short: "I've got it." I didn't want to be a burden to them. As long as I could, I would do everything for myself. I knew what it was like to walk, run, ride a bike, golf, play soccer and dance tap, jazz, and ballet. I couldn't allow myself to dwell on reality. I held onto the hope that my disease would stabilize and not progress. If I could walk by hanging onto the furniture, I was happy.

CHAPTER FOUR

Building a Mystery

My loneliness perpetuated. Two years had passed since I had graduated from high school and I needed a friend. A real friend who would love me unconditionally. A friend who would be happy to see me when we were together. A loyal friend who would stay by my side no matter what I experienced. In other words, I needed a dog. (And if that dog happened to be cute and cuddly with really long ears, I would consider it an added blessing.)

All I had to do was convince Mom. I knew she loved me with all her heart, but she wasn't too keen on the idea of having a dog in her house. With animals came messes, and her life was already stretched to the max. Every time I asked, she replied, "No! No! No!"

But I persisted and, over time, she softened. Why, I wasn't sure at first, but I've since learned that it was my horrible loneliness and need to have someone in my life that chipped away at her defenses. I understood her reasons for denying my request, but my longing never waned. Her tender heart eventually worked in my favor.

She told me I could have a little teeny tiny dog, one that weighed between eight and ten pounds. I was so excited that I immediately crawled upstairs to research dog breeds on the Internet with my sister Caitlin.

A few days passed before I sat down with my mom to go over my research. The first words out of my mouth were, "Mom, I've found the perfect dog breed for me!"

"Oh?"

"Yes," I said. "I want a dog that's low-key, one that will lie around and be my best friend."

"That sounds good."

"The one I want has long, droopy ears and a sad face. She's a porch dog, Mom."

"A porch dog?" Mom looked a bit confused, so I continued.

"I know all about the temperament of this breed." I filled her in on all the details, but I paused when I got to the part she wouldn't like. "There's only one problem," I said, the word "problem" hovering over me like a dark cloud.

Mom tried to urge me on. "What's the problem, Gabe?"

I held my breath. If she said that two-letter word my heart would break.

"When these dogs are full grown," I said, "they get between 60 and 100 pounds."

Her response was immediate and final. "No. No way. There is no way we are having a dog that large in the house, Gabe! It will never happen!" She turned and walked away.

I had gotten that far and couldn't let it go. I pestered her throughout the next few weeks, trying to convince her that this was the perfect dog for me. I said, "Mom, I love their face and long, droopy ears . . . " I begged and pleaded with her. Eventually I got up the nerve to ask, "Just do me a favor, Mom. Call the breeder I found online and ask her about the puppies. I want a little girl dog, one with the longest ears possible."

Mom still wasn't receptive to the breed, a coonhound, but she did pick up the phone and call the breeder. I dogged her the whole time she was on the phone, listening intently and interrupting often. "What's she saying, Mom? Ask her if she has one with long ears." I could hardly stand the suspense.

"Let me talk, Gabe. Let me talk. I'll tell you in a minute."

When Mom told her that she would give it some thought and get back with her, my heart raced. There was a chance!

After Mom got off the phone, she said, "Chris Hooker does happen to have a female puppy available, and she happens to have the longest ears in the litter." As if that weren't enough, she added that this puppy's "temperament is very mellow."

What more could I want?

My heart was overjoyed. Of course, Mom hadn't said I could have her yet, and I still had to get the idea past my mom's father, Papa, who lived with us. And then there was my stepfather, too.

Caitlin knew the dog would be good for me, so she stood by me throughout my quest. She even helped me break the news to Papa and Rick.

Papa shook his head and rolled his eyes, but Rick was adamantly against having a dog and quickly said, "No Way!"

I kept pestering him, but it wasn't until Mom told him she thought the dog would be good for me and give me purpose that he began to soften. She even went so far as to say that she'd make me take full responsibility for the dog. I would be held accountable for the dog in every way. I would not only have to pay for her, but I would be responsible for her needs and care.

Mom said, "Just like you're my daughter, this dog will be your little girl. You'll be physically and financially responsible for her. When the puppy has to go to the vet for anything, I'll drive you to the vet, but you have to take her in and do all the talking. Even if the puppy needs to go outside in the middle of the night, you'll have to crawl to the back door and do it yourself, Gabe."

Although it sounded like Mom was being cruel, she had my best interest at heart. She knew the movement would be good for my muscles and help to force me out of the cocoon I put myself in. All I knew was that I wanted this puppy, and I would agree to do anything if it meant I could have her.

At this point, the breeder knew nothing about my disability. When Mom called Chris back, she told the breeder she had been thinking about the puppy and wanted to be sure the dog wouldn't be too overpowering for me when it was full grown. She then explained that I had a progressive neuro-muscular disease, but left out some details. Chris was unaware of my aversion to wheelchairs.

Chris was quick to reassure her. "No, this dog is mellow," she said. "She'll be fine."

Mom and Chris agreed before they hung up, that this puppy and I would be a good match.

After their phone conversation, Mom hung up and told me, "The female puppy Chris has with the longest ears in the litter will be yours, Gabe."

I was stoked.

A day or so later the phone rang, and I answered it. I was shocked to find Chris Hooker on the other end of the line. Since Mom knew how I felt about her telling others about my disease, I was surprised when Chris said she was concerned about letting her puppy come to our home without knowing whether or not I was in a wheelchair. Chris was very particular about who she let adopt her dogs. She didn't hesitate to say, "I can't let the puppy come to your house unless there's a wheelchair in it, Gabe. Puppies need to grow up around wheels, or they'll become fearful of them. When the puppy gets bigger, I don't want her to be afraid to walk beside you."

The thought of getting a wheelchair, made me want to vomit, but I was willing to do anything—even that—to make this puppy mine.

When Mom came home I told her about my conversation with Chris. She was surprised to see that I hadn't gone off the deep end. She knew how I felt about her telling anyone about my condition. I still refused to let anyone in the house mention anything that had to do with my disease. Since Chris knew nothing about my two-year evasion of adaptive equipment, Mom was shocked to discover I was even entertaining the thought of having a wheelchair in the house. My desperate longing to have a best friend outweighed all else.

My willingness to cooperate and get a wheelchair sealed the deal. Chris agreed to let me adopt her female puppy and I could plan for her arrival. Although I told Mom the wheelchair wasn't for me, but for the puppy, she didn't push me. My consent to have one in the house was a huge enough breakthrough.

While I'd agreed to have a wheelchair in the house, I hadn't agreed to cooperate with the purchase. The grim day came to order my wheelchair and my mood was dark.

The saleswoman tried to get me to review her catalog. She needed me to tell her what I wanted. And that was the problem. I didn't want a wheelchair. I didn't want to have one or want to need one any more than I wanted Friedreich's ataxia in the first place. She did not seem to understand where I was coming from. And how could she? She had no need for the chairs she was selling. To her, they were only chairs. To me, they were banners that announced, "Look at me! I'm disabled." To her, they were tools that would help me get around. To me, they were hard evidence that I had given in to my disease.

I couldn't even bring myself to look at the lady, never mind listen to her suggestions. She said, "Pick out something fun." What was wrong with her? Couldn't she see that there was nothing fun about a wheelchair? I wanted to blend in, not stand out.

We placed the order as quickly as we could and left.

When the wheelchair arrived, it sat in our dining room folded up. I threw a blanket over it, unable to even look at it. That wheelchair was for the puppy, not for me. I promised to buy the chair, not use it. To me, it was just one more item to check off my to-do list before the puppy arrived. I could still walk if I hung onto the tables, walls, or anything else in my path, so why should I use a chair? I couldn't give in. I equated the wheelchair with giving up—and I could never give up.

Was it wrong for me to want to walk forever?

It wasn't long before my mother tried to lure me into using the chair. We could go shopping together, she'd say. Or to lunch. Or to a movie. We could go anywhere now that we had the chair. Knowing she was not the least bit ashamed of me was huge. She only pressured me to get out of the house and enjoy life again.

Still, I refused her invites. Sure, I would let her be my walker, so I could get to the car, but I would only ride along with her on errands. I wouldn't get out of the van. I couldn't.

I prepared for my new puppy like an expectant mother planning for a new baby. Mom even entertained the idea of giving me a puppy shower, but with her busy work schedule, we couldn't fit it in.

In my desire to be well prepared, I asked Chris numerous questions. I wanted to be sure she would have everything she needed before it was time for her to leave her birth mother, Faye, and come live with me, her new mommy. The list Chris gave me of supplies I would need kept me busy enough shopping and searching the Internet. The realization that I was finally going to have my own little girl to care for and love increased with every package that arrived at my door. Staying in the van was no longer an option as some things my new arrival needed could only be picked up in local stores.

About a month before my puppy was to arrive, I got a call from Chris. She was in the process of filling out her registration papers. My baby would need a name. Because my dog was so much smaller than the other puppies, Chris had referred to her at the kennel as Itty Bitty. But I needed to choose a name for the American Kennel Club (AKC) registry.

The AKC registers purebred dogs and their registered names need to follow specific guidelines. Registered names can only have so many characters and the AKC limits the number of dogs that can have the same name. As a result, owners naming dogs sometimes need to be creative. Chris wanted my dog's litter to be named after song titles. She said, "The father, Bruce, is named as a tribute to Bruce Springsteen. His registered name is CH Foxfire *Born in the U.S.A.* I don't care if it's a country song, rock and roll, religious, or whatever, but let me know what you come up with." For a couple of weeks I listened intently to songs on the radio. *Building a Mystery* by Sarah McLachlan was popular at the time and I heard it often. It didn't take me long to decide that this would be my dog's AKC registered name.

Then there was the call name to think about, the name that we would use every day. Although it would have made sense for me to just call her Sarah, I wanted her call name to be more unusual—just like she was. I enjoyed watching a weekly show at the time called *Roswell*, a science fiction drama about a spaceship that supposedly crashed on a farm in Roswell, New Mexico. A lead character's name was Isobel. While I liked her name, I wanted it to be even more unusual, so I scoured baby books to find a unique spelling. I ended up using Sarah Izabel as her call name, Izzy for short.

When the long awaited arrival day came, my twentieth birthday was just four days away. What a gift my Izzy would be! The excitement escalated as Caitlin, my youngest sister Madeline, Mom, and I packed up the hunter green van we rented for the trip and headed down to Ashtabula, Ohio. Bob Urban, Izzy's co-breeder, had picked up my new puppy from Chris Hooker in Sanford, North Carolina, and he was meeting us there.

My family, waiting like the expectant parents we were, arrived before Bob with Craig and Sharon Akin, a couple from Michigan who were also picking up a puppy. We knew the minute Bob arrived, because when he pulled up in front of the hotel room, we could hear the dogs and puppies whining.

My heart raced in anticipation. Bob came into the room to introduce himself, and while it was great to meet him, all I could think about was Izzy. I could hardly wait to meet my little girl. What would it be like to finally hold my puppy?

I didn't have long to wait. All the new doggie parents went out to his vehicle and peered in at the dogs. Among his full-grown coonhounds were the three puppies, Alice, Grace, and Izzy. My fingers itched to touch her, but Bob suggested that we return to the hotel. He would bring them in there.

I sat in a chair when he placed my little girl in my arms. My heart instantly overflowed. It was definitely love at first sight. Her ears were perfect—long and velvety. My thoughts exclaimed in delight: "*She's finally mine!*"

The size of her paws amazed me. They were huge in comparison to her size. Her belly was warm and soft. Holding her to my face, I kissed her on the top of her head. How could I resist?

When I put her on the floor and watched her walk, her little tail stuck straight up, and I noticed the cute little brown patch on her bottom. We gave her water from the pink dish Chris had sent along. She drained the bowl and carried it around in her mouth as if asking for a refill. She was adorable.

My mom, sisters, and I played with her on the bed for some time when we realized how late it was getting. As much as I hated to put her in the crate, I knew she would be safer traveling in it. After her crate was tucked into the back of the van, we headed home.

A half-hour into the trip, Izzy started crying. Although we tried talking to her, she would not settle down. When we could stand it no longer, Mom pulled over and went to get her. The minute she placed her in my lap, the crying ceased. I was amazed at how quickly we bonded.

Mom couldn't resist reaching over and rubbing her soft webbed feet. Teasing, she asked, "Are you sure this is the dog you want? If she's not, we can turn around and take her back."

I didn't realize she was teasing and said, "Oh, I'm sure this is the perfect dog for me." In my opinion, Izzy and I made a perfect match.

Mom tired after several hours on the road, so we pulled over, climbed into the back, and took a nap. Unfortunately, Izzy wasn't tired at all. In fact, she took advantage of her unsupervised time and began a complete investigation of the van. Like the raccoons her breed was known to hunt, she made a fine mess of everything.

When we arrived home in the middle of the night with the newest addition to the family, we were exhausted. Caitlin, Madeline and I snuggled with Izzy on my bed and slept for hours.

Mom told me she had tip-toed into my room the next morning to check on us. For a time, she stood gazing at her three sleeping beauties, with my new little girl snuggled in the center of us. This was Izzy's first day at her new home, and already Mom could see how good she would be for all of us. Her heart was overjoyed.

It took a while for us to settle into a routine, but I adored Izzy and was willing to do anything for her—even crawling outside in the middle of the night to let her potty.

Izzy hadn't been with us for long when I began to notice her sluggishness. I couldn't put my finger on it, but something wasn't quite right.

I put my worries aside, but still I watched her closely. The weather was warmer than usual for early spring, so Mom and I sat on the back porch while Izzy played with Madeline and Caitlin. Because I couldn't run with her, I loved watching her interact with my sisters. I noticed right away that she didn't seem to have much energy. She eventually found her way to the porch to lie on her mattress and sleep. At first I didn't think too much about it, but when a car backfired so loudly it made all of us jump and Izzy didn't even budge, my concerns escalated. Mom noticed her lack of response as well, so I asked, "Mom, what's wrong with Izzy? Is my little girl deaf?"

She immediately tried to wake her, but it didn't work. I asked her to call Chris, who wasn't too concerned, considering all the new changes that had taken place in Izzy's life. Puppies, she reminded us, do sleep a lot during the day, so again we blew it off.

Little did we know that this would only be the first of many unexplainable incidents that would eventually cause Izzy to live up to her registered name— Foxfire *Building a Mystery*.

"NO SCHOOL BULLYING!"

Gabe and Izzy Publishing

CHAPTER FIVE

The Liver Shunt

That first night with Izzy, when Mom checked up on us girls cuddling with Izzy, she glanced at the snow globe I kept on my dresser. I'd picked it up at Disney World when I turned four. It was a Goofy-themed snowglobe featuring Mickey's best friend dressed like a pirate. She wound the key on the base and the tune *Yo Ho!* (*A Pirate's Life For Me)* broke the silence. The song sparked a whirlwind of joyful memories in her mind. It also sparked an idea. We would take a family vacation to Disney World.

A trip that I wouldn't be going on. Going to Disney World meant using a wheelchair. I couldn't do that. Mom believed the chair would give me back my freedom, and she wanted that for me more than anything. But still I refused to go.

Mom was on a mission. She sent away for a Disney video and theme park pamphlets. She played the video for my sisters. I didn't join them, nor did I share in their excitement.

Still, I could hear the lyrics to several Disney tunes through my bedroom walls. *Yo Ho!* (*A Pirate's Life For Me)* was one of my favorite songs. Mom knew how much I loved Goofy—and that I was convinced a coonhound, like my Izzy, had inspired his character. Memories of my favorite Disney character Goofy and his long droopy ears began to tug at my heart.

Mom was persistent. It will be fun, Gabe. You'll love it, Gabe. We'll all be together. And no one knew me in Florida, so it wouldn't matter if I had to use the chair. She didn't ask for an answer right away. She simply asked me to think about it.

I watched my two little sisters closely throughout the next few weeks. They couldn't stop talking about the trip, asking questions about rides and what they'd see. Their excitement was contagious.

Mom had one more trick up her sleeve. If we drove to Florida, we also could stop off in North Carolina on the way back home and meet Chris Hooker, Izzy's breeder. There, I could meet Izzy's daddy Bruce (Foxfire *Born in the U.S.A.*), her mommy Faye (Foxfire *Fayalite*), and her brother Ben (Foxfire *Stand By Me*). Now I was intrigued. I already loved Izzy. I couldn't miss meeting her furry family.

I finally told Mom I would go.

Departure day had finally arrived. As soon as our van was packed and my chair was secured in the back, we headed toward Florida. I hated leaving Izzy at the kennel, but Mom assured me that she would be okay and the people at the kennel were kind. When they said I could call and check up on her, I breathed a huge sigh of relief. The 19-hour journey south seemed to take forever, but when we arrived in Orlando and saw the Disney World sign, the long car ride was suddenly worthwhile.

We planned to visit Disney World first, then Sea World. Disney World was everything I had remembered and then some. Being there with my sisters, Mom, and Rick only added to my joy. It was a blast. Disney World's atmosphere is magical and happy. It's a place where I feel accepted and don't worry about being ridiculed or judged. I went on most of the rides at the park, with Pirates of the Caribbean being my favorite. I was uneasy about being at the park in my chair but everyone treated me well at Disney World. It was so different than life back at school. It was amazing.

Unfortunately, for me, Sea World was a different story.

Caitlin, Rick, and I waited in line for the water coaster Journey to Atlantis. Wheelchair-bound people were supposed to enter the ride in a different area. As I approached the entrance, I asked the attendant where I should go. The attendant seemed a bit annoyed and was very rude to me. She even rolled her eyes. I took it personally. Would she have done that if I were not disabled? If I were not in a chair? Had I not been sensitive already about the chair, I might have handled her reaction differently. Overall, her timing stunk.

Irritated, I left the entrance and wheeled back to where Mom waited for us at the ride's end. She could tell I was upset but wanted to make sure I still enjoyed the vacation. Don't let this one incident ruin your whole day, Gabe. Just blow it off and forget her.

"*Didn't she understand?* I thought. Inconsolable, my tears quickly turned to uncontrollable sobs. People gawked. I hated being on display, but I could not regain my composure. I thought, "*Is this how people in wheelchairs are treated?*" If so, I wanted no part of it.

She said, "The Shamu Show is about to start. Let's head that way." The Shamu show? I'd need to sit in a designated area for wheelchairs and be separated from my family. I'd feel even more different, more separate. No thank you. I refused to go.

Mom was determined that the family enjoy the trip. She said, "Okay, if you don't want to go, and you can't shrug this off, meet the rest of us at the park exit at five o'clock. I'm not going to let this day be ruined for Caitlin and Madeline."

She'd always told me that she wouldn't disable me more than my condition already had. She'd always treated me like any other kid. Still, I was surprised. In a bit of a fog, I watched my family walk away and spent the rest of my day at Sea World alone. Unaccustomed to my wheelchair, I found it difficult to navigate, so I mostly sat around and people watched. A lady came up to me and offered sunscreen. In the direct sun, my legs and nose had begun to burn. The hat I had on wasn't protecting my nose, and since I had shorts on, my legs were exposed.

Without a cell phone, I couldn't contact my family to catch up with them. The solitude gave me time to think. Rick and Mom had spent a great deal of money on the tickets to get into Sea World, and my anger spoiled the day for all of them. What happened to me earlier was wrong, but that didn't give me the right to spoil everyone else's fun.

At 5 p.m., I rolled up to the gate where Mom had said to meet them. I saw my family approaching and I began to smile. Mom asked, "Are you sorry you spent the day alone, Gabe?"

"Yes!" I emphatically stated. I told her that I had wanted to contact her throughout the day, but that I hadn't been able to. Mom is very sensitive, and I knew how hard it must have been for her to leave me alone in that giant park, but I learned some valuable lessons from the experience.

As glad as I was to get back to the hotel and rest, I longed to go home and see my Izzy. Although I missed her terribly, I kept my longing inside. The trip wasn't over yet. In the morning, we would pack and head back. Our plan to stop overnight in Sanford, North Carolina to meet Chris and Izzy's family filled me with wonder as the miles that separated us lessened.

We arrived on schedule and went to the hotel to unload our luggage before calling Chris. The plan was to meet her and her husband, Terry, at his favorite seafood restaurant. Although I was excited about meeting them, I was nervous as well. I could only hope she would like me. After all, I was raising one of her puppies.

All my apprehensions disappeared the moment I met them. They were both nice, and it didn't take long for them to figure out just how much Izzy had impacted my life. She meant the world to me.

After dinner, we went out for ice cream before visiting the veterinarian hospital where Chris worked. She needed to check on the dogs. We were taking a tour of the office when Chris handed me a new mulberry-colored dog collar. She grinned and said, "It's for Izzy from Grandma Hooker."

I laughed out loud. This was only the beginning of a long-lasting relationship with Chris, known better to my family as Izzy's Grandma Hooker.

The next day, while Caitlin and I stayed with Chris and the dogs, Mom, Rick, and Madeline went to Charleston to the plantation where the television mini-series *North and South* had been filmed. For them, this was a must see. Not only was this Mom's favorite mini-series, but she also had named Madeline after one of the characters. At only four years old, Madeline somehow believed the plantation was actually hers. They took her photo in front and she realized it was a tourist destination years later.

Meeting Izzy's family was fun. She got her long body and short front legs from her mother Faye, but she looked more like her daddy Bruce in the face. She definitely had his attitude. Bruce didn't think twice about barking at the other dogs. He acted like he was top coonhound, where Faye was mellow and sweet. As time has passed, I've seen both personalities in Izzy.

Her brother Ben was huge. He had loads of energy and a playfulness that surprised me, especially considering how mellow Izzy was. He was definitely a lover boy. Like Izzy, he loved to get up on the sofa and snuggle, but he took it one step further and wanted to sit on our laps—as if a dog his size could ever be a lap dog!

As much as I enjoyed our trip, I couldn't wait to get to the kennel to pick up my Izzy girl. They say that absence makes the heart grow fonder. While I never would have believed I could love Izzy more than I already did, this day the phrase rang true for me. When my eyes met hers, I felt an incredible bond. We were overjoyed to see each other.

Our outward show of affection told everyone in the room that our hearts were in sync. Her long ears swung back and forth as she trotted over to lick my face. After her warm greeting, Izzy lay down next to me so I could pet her belly. I wasn't surprised. This is one of our favorite pastimes at home. I would lie beside her on the rug and rub her belly for hours. It was so good to see her that I decided I never wanted to be apart from her for that long again.

On the car ride home to Fenton, Izzy curled up next to me and fell asleep. She was as peaceful as if she knew she was finally going home. Unfortunately, the observations from the woman at the kennel weighed heavily on my mind.

Mom had asked the woman, "How was she?"

The woman said, "She's not very active."

Mom probed. "What do you mean?"

The woman replied, "Izzy doesn't have the energy that most young puppies do. We were wondering if maybe you don't socialize her enough. She just didn't want to play with the other dogs and she wanted nothing to do with going for walks. She only wanted to sleep. That's really not normal."

She added, "You need to make sure she's spending enough time with people and other dogs, or you're not going to have a very happy dog."

Did they think I didn't take good care of Izzy? I felt instantly protective of my little girl.

At home, Rick helped me give Izzy a bath. She was dirty and had formed sores on her elbows from sleeping on the kennel's cement floor. Even her shiny, velvety coat had dulled since we had dropped her off.

Mom and I agreed that we would never kennel her again. If we needed to go somewhere and she couldn't go, we'd get one of our friends to take care of her. I was heartbroken to see my beautiful friend looking so bedraggled.

Still, the kennel's observations concerned us. We made an appointment with her veterinarian, Dr. Sandy Smith, to get her opinion on Izzy's condition. After giving us medication for her elbows, Dr. Smith sent us on our way, saying that Izzy seemed fine otherwise.

She was fine? She didn't seem fine. That evening I couldn't sleep and watched Izzy restless in her crate. She fussed and couldn't seem to get comfortable. She circled and pressed her head against the crate wall. We tried to comfort her. Eventually, by rubbing her belly, we soothed her into sleep. But something was still wrong the next day. She spat up, was lethargic and slept most of the day.

We called the breeder, Chris, but she wasn't too worried. She reminded us that puppies do sleep a lot and suggested that maybe Izzy ate something that upset her belly.

It made sense to Mom and me. We wanted the answer to be that simple. Feeling somewhat relieved after talking to Chris, we decided to give Izzy a day or so to recover before seeking medical help.

Izzy had other ideas. That evening Mom and Rick left for dinner and a movie. I was home alone with Izzy. The night seemed peaceful until Izzy suddenly began to retch and struggle, as if she were choking. Thinking her collar was too tight, I quickly cut it free with a pair of scissors. I called Mom to explain what was happening. She and Rick came right home.

We sat together in the kitchen that night watching Izzy. One minute she would seem fine, and the next she was restless, coughing and walking into walls. The efforts would exhaust her and she'd fall asleep in her crate. Not willing to leave my little girl's side, I lay on the hardwood floor beside her for the entire night.

Early the next morning, something went terribly wrong. Without thought for my sleeping family, I yelled out, "Mom!"

She and Rick flew down the stairs. My tone told them something was seriously wrong. Izzy lay lifeless. She was unable to move, never mind stand.

Normally at this time of morning, I was letting her outside. Not today— today my little girl was in dire straits.

Mom called Dr. Smith, who told her to bring Izzy in immediately. After x-rays, Dr. Smith informed us that Izzy had ingested a large rock and would need surgery right away. She suggested we go home and she would call us to let us know how Izzy was doing.

Although I was reluctant to leave, I knew she was in good hands. The surgery removed the rock but Dr. Smith noticed that Izzy was not coming out of anesthesia as quickly as she should have.

She asked us to come back to the office and try to awaken her. Dr. Smith knew how much I loved Izzy and thought my touch and the sound of my voice might help. As I talked to Izzy, I rubbed my fingers down her long, velvety ears. It wasn't long before Izzy began to wake up. While going over post-op instructions, Dr. Smith told us that she suspected Izzy had a liver shunt.

A liver shunt! The words alone caused the beat of my heart to increase tenfold. Although I didn't know what a liver shunt was, it didn't sound good. Again and again, I thought, *"Why my dog?"*

Dr. Smith told me exactly what I needed to watch for with a liver shunt. After she gave me Izzy's post-op medication, we took her home.

At first I couldn't accept that something was wrong with my little girl. As much as I trusted Dr. Smith, I believed that once I got her home she would be okay.

Mom told me not to worry but to wait and see how she did in the next few weeks. That is what I did.

Unfortunately, it wasn't long before Izzy began displaying symptoms again. Dr. Smith's suspicions were becoming a reality. Izzy was diagnosed with a portal systemic shunt (commonly called a liver shunt). This condition allows some of her blood to flow back into the circulatory system before being detoxified by the liver. When toxins build up in the brain, they can cause neurological symptoms. Izzy's balance and coordination problems were results of the liver shunt. Little did we know this was just the beginning of her health issues.

Watching her stagger and stumble around brought back memories of my own progressive condition. No doubt about it, Izzy's condition mirrored mine.

Major surgery to correct the condition was recommended. Another surgery? My poor Izzy!

When I told Mom I wanted a dog, I had to agree to pay for all the expenses involved in raising her. Mom was already stretched to the limit, and she could not afford the added expense at the time. I was twenty, so how could I ask her to help after I agreed to be held accountable?

Although I had no problem agreeing to her terms, I never entertained the thought of my dog needing extensive surgery. Still, I tried to keep my word. It wasn't easy, but Dr. Smith was the best.

I managed to pay for the surgery to remove Izzy's rock, and Dr. Smith was nice enough to let me set up a payment plan for all the tests related to the liver shunt. Unfortunately, that was only the beginning of the treatments and costs.

Not only did she need a second surgery, she would have to have regular exams to monitor her condition.

Dr. Smith, however, could not perform liver shunt surgery. I had no choice but to look for a surgeon who would accept a payment plan.

There were no guarantees that this would be the end of Izzy's surgeries. New expenses accrued all the time, becoming a real strain on me. I had no choice but to ask Mom for help.

Unfortunately, she had just paid for us to go to Florida. The timing was horrible. Her heart broke for me, but she didn't have the money to give. She offered to do a home equity loan on our house, but when she checked into it, the bank told her she hadn't been in the house long enough.

"Gabe," she reminded me, "I told you before you got Izzy that you were in charge of her care. Izzy is your responsibility in the same way you and your sisters are mine."

If I didn't find someone to help me, my dog would die. I couldn't give up on her. Izzy meant the world to me.

Mom knew all too well what it was like to feel helpless. She had been there many times with me. Giving up was not an option. Mom's heart ached for me—and for Izzy.

Out of her desperate desire to help, she said, "Let me call Uncle Clayton. I'll ask him if he has any suggestions. If nothing else, we can gather together as a family and see if there's anything we can do." Hope rose within me. Mom planned to call him the next day after she had given everything we discussed some thought.

Uncle Clayton suggested a fundraiser.

"A fundraiser!" Mom exclaimed. "Absolutely not! No way! Gabe does not take charity!" He told Mom this wasn't about her; it was about me needing help for my dog. He also told her that she needed to swallow her pride and let me accept the help I desperately needed. Mom was humbled by his words. I liked my uncle's idea because it would help Izzy. After much thought, Mom finally agreed.

Uncle Clayton contacted his friend Kim Crawford. When Kim called, he asked Mom if he could come out to the house and visit with Izzy and me. He wanted to interview me. Mom agreed, assuming the interview was part of the fundraising process. It wasn't until Kim arrived at our home that we found out he was from the *Flint Journal* newspaper.

At first Mom wasn't too pleased, but neither was she willing to turn him away. After all, he was taking the time to help us help Izzy. Mom was a bit confused, though. She thought Uncle Clayton had contacted his friend to help set up a fundraiser, not write a newspaper article.

The story was titled *Gabe and Izzy Lean on Each Other to Survive Tragic Disease.* When the paper hit the stands, Mom received a phone call from one of her former classmates and friend, Linda Widing. She wanted to organize a fundraiser for me, but Mom's immediate response was, "No!" Clearly, mom had not totally embraced the idea of a fundraiser. Mom and I had no way of knowing what would be in the newspaper article Kim offered to write or what would follow. I must admit the interview was fun. It was all about Izzy. And if I'm not mistaken, Kim enjoyed our little chat as well.

The response to Kim's article was amazing. So many offered to help that I was able to pay off Izzy's balance at Dr. Smith's. Unfortunately, Izzy's condition was ongoing, so her bills continued to accumulate.

Linda had a strong desire to help others and was not about to take no for an answer. She told Mom that people like to help those in need so Mom hesitantly agreed to let her proceed.

Linda hit the ground running. She arranged to place fundraising canisters throughout our town in banks and local veterinarian offices. The canisters helped immensely. One man made a donation of $1,000! My heart was over-whelmed by everyone's generosity. The money would no sooner come in than

I'd drop it off at Dr. Smith's office. The day my vet bills were paid in full was a huge load off my mind. I couldn't have been happier.

Others found their own ways to help. Linden Elementary School took up donations. Julie Eichman, the mother of one of my sister's friends, helped as well. She was a Girl Scout leader and her troop made a generous contribution sent with a photo of the troop and a card signed by the girls. Some people in the town brought Izzy dog food, while others sent flowers and well wishes. There were so many that to list them all would take another book.

Receiving from others was not easy, but knowing those in my community and the surrounding communities cared about Izzy meant so much to me. Our family slowly learned that while it is better to give than receive, when we aren't willing to receive from others, we rob those giving of the blessing they receive when giving from their hearts.

Linda and others taught Mom and me that it's okay to accept help when you need it. Swallowing our pride was not easy, but it was necessary to get the help Izzy needed. While I was still afraid of being seen by former classmates who made fun of me, knowing Izzy needed me caused me to put my fears aside. A new sense of community was being born in my heart. People gathered together, bound by a good cause. I was astounded by the response.

Being open to help took us on a journey that seemed lined with happy accidents. We knew that these events were too good to be merely happenstance. These were our blessings.

Izzy's medical needs continued to build. Mom called number after number to find a surgeon who would accept a payment plan for the second surgery. She called the Michigan State University Veterinarian Clinic to check on the cost of this type of surgery. The lady in the business office told Mom it would be $2,000 to drop Izzy off, and it could cost another $2,000 to pick her up. This would have been a huge burden on me. Although Mom tried to negotiate a payment plan, the woman told her it didn't matter if I had good credit or not, they simply did not offer payment plans.

I could hear Mom crying while she was on the phone. Before she hung up, she told the woman she would find help for her daughter one way or another.

By then, Sharon Akin, the owner of Izzy's sisters, had heard about Izzy's condition. She called a TV station in Detroit to see if their viewers or staff knew of any veterinarian specialists who accepted payment plans. Shortly thereafter, Mom received a call from the station's anchorwoman, Leslie LoBue. Leslie was an animal lover herself. Through her contacts she found us a veterinarian in Bloomfield Hills, only an hour away, who would do the surgery for free!

For free? It seemed too good to be true.

Mom was quick to tell Leslie, "Absolutely not! We're not looking for charity, just a payment plan for Gabe." Mom knew that her pride was getting in the way again, but she was adamant.

However, Leslie had the jump on her. The doctor had already made it clear to Leslie that he would not do the surgery unless we accepted it as a donation.

Mom's shoulders slumped. Here this doctor wanted to bless us, and she was going to rob him of the blessing he'd receive for doing it. When Leslie mentioned that Dr. Riggs was the name of the vet who would do the surgery, Mom began to laugh. We happened to live on Riggs Street. Was it a coincidence? Or a reminder of our blessings?

I later learned there would be many additional expenses, such as x-rays, medicines, overnight expenses, and other costs that were not included in the surgery. We would still have the opportunity to pay our share.

On the way to the see Dr. Riggs for a consultation, Sarah McLachlan's song *Building a Mystery*—the very one for which Izzy was named—played on the radio. Another wonderful coincidence!

When the day arrived for her surgery, I dressed her in a Detroit Red Wings dog T-shirt for good-luck. I had been an avid fan of the Detroit Red Wings since I was a young girl attending the Stanley Cup Championship parades. We loved the team and hoped their strength would help Izzy through this surgery.

Sarah McLachlan's song couldn't have been more appropriate. Izzy's condition was a mystery. Though Dr. Riggs believed the shunt was on the outside of Izzy's liver (a scenario with an eighty percent survival rate), when he later opened her up he could not find it. The shunt's location was a mystery. The shunt had to be somewhere deep inside her liver. This particular surgery would be incredibly difficult requiring more tests and additional surgery.

Dr. Riggs closed Izzy up and planned to discuss her medical condition at an upcoming veterinarian convention in Washington, D.C. After the convention, he would call me to let me know what the next step for Izzy would be.

A day after Izzy came home, her bandage was full of drainage. Mom had worked a long day, but when she got home, I asked her to look at Izzy's dressing. She was worried and called Oakland Veterinary Referral Services (OVRS), an after-hours emergency clinic, and spoke with a veterinary technician. We were told to bring Izzy in immediately for an examination.

It was dark outside when Mom and Rick helped me get Izzy into the van. The hour-long ride to the clinic in Bloomfield Hills gave me too much time to think. I was terrified I would lose Izzy.

When we arrived, the emergency room was full, so we signed in and waited our turn. Mom and Rick looked exhausted. It would be a long night and they both had to work the next day. Still, they didn't want Izzy to suffer either. They loved Izzy almost as much as I did.

Her incision hadn't closed properly and Izzy was readmitted to the hospital. The next day we discovered that she wasn't responding to the IV medications and would need blood from a donor dog. Later that day we learned that a donor dog had arrived that was the perfect match. It was Barkley, Leslie LoBue's yellow lab. Leslie had no idea that Izzy had been readmitted. She'd merely taken her dog to donate blood at the clinic's blood bank. It was another blessing. Izzy was home in less than twenty-four hours, all thanks to what we called her "Barkley Booster."

Dr. Riggs called after he returned from his convention and told Mom that he discussed Izzy's case with a number of his colleagues. It was determined that Michigan State University had the equipment needed to locate the liver shunt. Mom was asked to call the dean of the Michigan State University-Center of Veterinary Medicine (MSU CVM). After her initial conversation with the school, she was concerned about the costs. They wouldn't accept a payment plan and that was the only way we could afford it. However, the dean read the article about Izzy in the *Flint Journal* and wanted to help. This surgery would be a good one for his students on which to learn. He told Mom not to worry about the expenses.

A few days later, a student veterinary technician called us about a special radioisotope test. They would inject a dye into Izzy to locate the shunt. They had a cancellation and wanted us to bring Izzy right over.

The drive to Lansing would take an hour and unfortunately the roads were covered with ice from a storm the night before. It was a white-knuckle drive. We inched along the freeway, warily observing trucks fishtailing and cars sliding into ditches. It was a harrowing drive but when *Building a Mystery* played on the radio—again—Mom and I both had felt chills run up and down our arms. We smiled and looked at each other. The timing was perfect.

We left Izzy in Lansing for her test and sat anxiously back home for the test results. The phone finally rang, and we learned Michigan State could not do the test to locate the shunt due to Izzy's large size. The amount of radioisotope that would be needed to locate the shunt exceeded the amount that the State of Michigan would allow them to inject in any dog. Their only alternative would be to cut into Izzy's liver, but they would only give her a fifty-fifty chance of surviving the procedure. Izzy had gone from an eighty percent to a fifty percent chance of survival.

When I heard this, I threw my hands in the air and said, "Bring her home! I don't want her dying on the table."

Mom and I drove back to Lansing to bring Izzy home. I had no way of knowing what her prognosis would be, but I could hardly wait to see her, comfort her, and rub her long, soft ears. They advised us to adjust her diet since Izzy's liver could not handle protein. We put her on a special prescription dog food that worked wonders, Hills Prescription Diet k/d, formulated especially to support a canine's kidney health. She gained back the thirty pounds she had lost, and Dr. Riggs started calling her a "Miracle Dog."

I started to call her my feisty fighter because she's just like me. Mom, however, stood her ground and still calls her "Angel Izzy," believing she was meant for me.

Not long after her recovery, I decided to have a professional photo taken of Izzy and me together. When we arrived at the studio, there was a photo on the wall of a little girl wearing angel wings.

It was perfect.

I knew Mom would be thrilled if I placed angel wings on Izzy for the photo. You see, in so many ways, Mom was right—Izzy was an angel to me.

Izzy's illness had forced me to push beyond my fears and limitations to help her. Mom wisely refused to do this for me. Therefore, I had to get out of the house and speak to the different veterinarians and their staffs myself.

My love for Izzy had drastically altered my path. My wheelchair became a necessity. How else could I get Izzy to her appointments at OVRS in Bloomfield Hills? Although I didn't like to use handicapped parking, Izzy needed to be close to the building. I set my own feelings aside and did everything I could to help her.

Because of Izzy, I formed relationships with surgeons, their staff, and many others. My fear of running into those who had bullied me was fading. And, somewhere along the line, the terrible loneliness that had been eating me up inside had started slowly dissipating. As if Izzy hadn't done enough for me already, she opened new doors for me to build friendships.

Her illness continued to force me out of hiding. I used to ask, "Why my dog?" No more. As the mystery continues to unfold, I see clearly that it *had* to be my dog that was sick. Otherwise, I would still be trapped within the walls of my self-made prison. Izzy helped me see I had only been in a cocoon waiting for my moment to fly.

Only time will tell how high.

CHAPTER SIX

Landing on Animal Planet

"I Will. Not. Do. It." I enunciated every word.

Mom threw her hands in the air and stormed out of the room. She had every right to be upset with me. The crew from Animal Planet was scheduled to film in two days, and I was a mess. Desperately, she wanted me to put my fears aside and do this, but how could I? My fears made perfect sense—to me. How could I talk about my disease on national television when I couldn't even talk to my family about it? At the same time, how could I let everyone down? In utter turmoil, I curled up on my bed in a fetal position, something I hadn't done since my pre-Izzy depression days.

Animal Planet had contacted me through the American Black and Tan Coonhound Club about my relationship with Izzy. The network had seen an article about me that ran in a local paper and that was picked up by the Associated Press. The breeder was excited. Mom was thrilled. I wasn't so sure.

Izzy and I were both a year older. Thinking about my time with my beloved Izzy, I could not and would not deny how much she had changed my life. I knew how much she had done for me. Could I do this for her?

It was January 8, 2001. The freezing temperatures outside were a true depiction of how I felt inside. However, the bright morning sun peeking through the blinds was a complete contradiction to my turbulent mood. Little by little, the winter glow melted away the icy layer that had formed around my wounded heart. As it did, my thoughts cleared.

I had wavered for days about whether I would appear on *A Pet Story*, a show on the Animal Planet television network. I'd been at odds with everyone—primarily with Mom, but also with other family members who were convinced the experience would be good for me.

But I needed to make a decision. Mom didn't want the producer, Joe Zimmerman, and his crew to fly all the way to Michigan only to have me shut my bedroom door in their faces.

I still wouldn't talk about my condition. I knew little about my disease, mostly because I'd refused to read about it. I had myself convinced that talking and learning about Friedreich's ataxia would make me depressed. In truth, I'd go ballistic if anyone brought it up. I'd make a hasty retreat to my room and slam the door. Perhaps my actions were childish, but they were effective.

With Joe, I was different. We'd talked several times by phone and he had a special gift for putting me at ease. It was as if I had known him for years. He assured me often that the filming would be fun. Perhaps he was right? After all, I had always liked Animal Planet.

I couldn't sleep. I tossed and turned, unable to make a decision. True, I had spoken to a few local newspaper reporters about my relationship with Izzy, but that was different. This program would be televised nationally. People would see the way I walked, and people would hear the way I talked. Although I could still walk with someone holding on tightly to my waist or by using walls, furniture, or rails to steady me, I was unstable. Worse, I hated my voice—it sounded a little slurred and hollow to me. Would there be millions of people laughing at me now instead of just a bunch of hometown bullies?

Though I had second-guessed my decision to do the show, I finally agreed because I didn't want to let everyone down. My family was so excited. Joe was not in Michigan yet, but he had already spent so much time on this project. And I did agree to do the show in the first place. Little by little, I saw this for what it was: a great honor. I would appear on a network I loved and watched every chance I got. More than anything, I owed this to Izzy. I was healing on the inside because of her, and the love we shared was giving me the courage to let go of my fears and learn to live again.

The taping that January 2001 was a lot of fun for me and my family. The crew— Joe, cameraman Doug Hostetter, and sound engineer Doug Trevethan—were all cut-ups and went out of their way to put my family and me at ease. On one of the days we were filming, Joe stopped to help Mom sew straps on Caitlin's ballet shoes. In my mind, it took a secure man to do something like that, but he thought nothing of it. He, like the others, were just part of our family.

Joe was not only a character, he was quite the singer as well. He just happened to find out that when I was little, I was a tap dancing duck in my first recital. His rendition of *Sesame Street's Rubber Ducky You're the One* was hilarious. How could I keep from cracking up? Joe really did have a special gift for making others feel good about themselves.

Doug entertained us all with his spot-on imitations of Steve Irwin, the now-belated "Crocodile Hunter" and Animal Planet personality. Doug tackled Madeline as if she were an enraged crocodile while shouting one of Irwin's favorite expressions, "Ferocious! Ferocious!" (Although I never had the pleasure of meeting Irwin, my family and I, along with millions of other viewers, have deeply mourned his sudden death.)

The taping had its challenges, however. On the first day, they taped my morning routine with Izzy. They filmed me brushing my hair and applying one of my many shades of lipstick (I have an obsession with shopping for new colors) and I was anxious. Being filmed alone was tough enough. Having a camera in my face as I put on make-up was even worse. I was very self-conscious when people watched me do little things.

Joe started filming before I even realized that morning. When I became aware, I was afraid I'd drop my mascara or something. Unfortunately, the "dropsies" are a symptom of my condition. Fortunately, this application was smooth sailing.

That afternoon, they filmed Izzy and me at the Animal Health Clinic with Izzy's wonderful vet, Dr. Smith. However, as soon as we were out of the van, Izzy realized where she was. After all her trials, she associated the Animal Health Clinic with pain. In this regard, Izzy and I are very much alike. She hates going to the doctor as much as I do. Unlike me, however, she could run away when she wanted. On this day, Izzy bolted toward the road with five-year-old Madeline frantically clinging to Izzy's retractable leash.

The crew covered every aspect of my life and Izzy's. They interviewed Dr. Craig Riggs, the veterinarian who donated his surgical services, and Leslie LoBue, the newscaster who connected us with Dr. Riggs. They even interviewed one of my doctors in Flint and filmed a segment at Great Lakes Crossing, a mall where I like to shop. (At the mall they filmed me at one of my favorite restaurants, Alcatraz, with a few friends. The restaurant is decorated with memorabilia from the former prison on Alcatraz Island in San Francisco Bay, a place I'd always wanted to visit. When a waitress asked us what the cameras were for I teased her that I was a famous actress in a movie with Johnny Depp. She rightly didn't believe me.)

Chris, the breeder, flew in from North Carolina for the occasion. My family and Chris were filmed together watching an Animal Planet show called *Breed All About It*. This was a special about coonhounds like Izzy where one of the rangers interviewed was Bob Urban, the co-owner of Izzy's mother Faye.

The long days of tapings made us all fast friends. One day we had lunch with the crew at Applebee's. Joe kindly took Mom's place in assisting me into the restaurant by holding me tightly around the waist. I was moved by the gesture.

That comfort level made the last day of filming, the most powerful day, possible. Joe interviewed me in-depth at home. He asked all kinds of questions that were unrelated to Izzy and me. While I didn't get very specific, he asked me questions about my school days. I frequently had to hold back tears because I didn't want anyone feeling sorry for me, and I said as much on camera. I told Joe it had been devastating when the kids made fun of me in school.

His easy nature even convinced my mom to go on camera. The crew did not tell her she was going to be part of the story until a half hour before she was to be filmed. Suddenly the shoe was on the other foot. She was nervous. She had never been interviewed on camera before. Like *I* ever had!

As hard as she tried to embark on this new adventure with grace and poise, she stumbled. The crew shot retake after retake. Every time she'd make a mistake, Joe would shout, "Cut!" and the rest of the family would dissolve into gut-wrenching laughter. Finally, Joe ordered everyone out of the house except the crew and Mom. No one could blame him. When Joe was finally satisfied, he went around the kitchen table to where Mom stood and gave her a big hug, swinging her around till her feet came off the ground.

After all the filming was done, my family exchanged gifts with the crew-members. I gave each member a copy of the Disney movie *The Duke*. The dog star of the film just happened to be Izzy's half-uncle. She's also a distant relative to the coonhound who starred in the Michael J. Fox movie *Doc Hollywood*. Guess I shouldn't have been surprised when Izzy landed on Animal Planet. She did come from a bloodline of hound celebrities.

Joe gave me a zippered Animal Planet sweatshirt, which I have since worn out. Who knows, but maybe someday I'll get another one! Also, having heard about my addiction to chocolate, Joe couldn't resist bringing me a three-pound box of chocolates. We both admired Tom Hanks' performance in *Forrest Gump*, so I was not surprised when he said as he handed the box to me, "My momma always said, life is like a box a chocolates—you never know what you're gonna get."

When the crew was ready to leave Fenton, I couldn't bear to say goodbye. I just said, "See you later." Goodbyes are too final—and too painful for me.

The first airing of "Izzy and Gabe" was in April of 2001. Between 2001 and 2005, the segment aired more than sixty times. I was told it became one of the most popular *A Pet Story* episodes ever produced. I have never watched it but so many others have and told me how much they enjoyed it. I still can't bear to hear how FA progresses, the mortality rates, and other statistics, but I knew they would discuss it on the show. Yes, I address groups of up to twelve hundred as a motivational speaker now, but I still hate my voice as much as I did when the segment taped. I've come a long way from the high school girl who had speech class waived because of her speaking phobia. And while I've been able to accept assistance for walking, I'd rather not hear or watch myself on camera.

Response to the show was immediate. We were flooded with letters. These notes impressed me and my whole family.

> *I happened to catch your show in 2003 when I was recovering in the hospital from my seventh surgery to repair a hernia surgery that had gone wrong. The courage and determination that you displayed, as well as your statement that you don't want anyone to feel sorry for you, gave me the inspiration and strength to get through that time and all of my subsequent surgeries. Thank you so much for what you have done for me.*
>
> —Dan

Many other cards and letters were special to us as well, such as this one:

> *Dear Gabe,*
>
> *I was hit by a car in a mountain bike accident and not expected to live, never mind walk again. Hearing your story on Animal Planet inspired me to persevere. Not only can I walk, but I am now a Research Scientist.*
>
> *Thanks for your willingness to share your incredible story.*
>
> —Sean

These letters inspired us in 2003 to set up our Web site, www.gabeandizzy. com, to connect with these viewers directly.

While I wished those days of filming never would have come to an end, they did. Had they not, the show never would have aired and my life as a motivational speaker would never have started.

After all these years, I still keep in touch with the crew.

I sent Doug a talking bobble-head of Steve Irwin for his birthday that year. Doug mentioned that it's his favorite gift and that he takes it everywhere he goes. He calls him "Stevie," and he says that whenever he's feeling shy or tongue-tied, he presses the button on the doll and Stevie says what he is thinking. Among all Stevie's sayings, "Isn't she Gorgeous?" is Doug's personal favorite.

Joe keeps in touch as well. He sends me pictures of his wife and kids and keeps us posted about Doug and his adventures. I kept that candy box he gave me for years. When letters began pouring in from viewers, I stored them in that empty box—a constant reminder of this special time in my life.

"NO SCHOOL BULLYING!"

Gabe and Izzy Publishing

CHAPTER SEVEN

Not in My Wildest Dreams

I should have been more nervous, but my friends and family gave me strength. I sat in the elementary school library at Linden Elementary to give one of my first public presentations after appearing on Animal Planet. While I'd originally dreaded the thought of speaking to another class, I felt I couldn't cancel. Their teacher had been so moved by my story in the *Flint Journal* that he had his students raise money for Izzy's vet bills ($35, but every cent helped). They even made Izzy and me posters filled with encouraging messages. One poster encouraged me not to give up hope for Izzy. I couldn't let them down.

Being surrounded by so many familiar faces helped me more than I could have predicted. My mom's friend Linda was there as well as my sisters Caitlin and Madeline. Even Izzy was there. Since Halloween was drawing close, I'd dressed her in an orange-and-black pullover zippered jacket and we painted her toenails orange.

Once at the school, I saw a heartwarming handmade sign welcoming Izzy and me. I greeted the children in a regular chair, not wanting the children to see me in my wheelchair. The teacher even brought the children to me in small groups. The talks were intimate and special. They were even fun. It made me feel more comfortable, and it helped ease me into my new role as motivational speaker.

Still, I wasn't completely convinced visiting schools was for me. I didn't see myself as a speaker, just someone who had spoken to a handful of classes. Mom knew my reluctance and my anxiety. At this time, she even needed to prod me to attend birthday parties, like the one my sister Madeline had been invited to at Chuck E. Cheese's.

I didn't want to go to the party, but Caitlin, Madeline, and Mom convinced me to ride along. I had every intention of staying in the car. My normal excuse of not wanting to run into former classmates came to mind, but that wouldn't work this time. We were in Flint, and Mom was quick to remind me that no one would know me except our friends.

Finally, Mom reminded me that Peggy, the birthday girl's grandmother, would be thrilled to see me. I relented. In high school, I used to go over to Peggy's house with my best friend, Amanda, who helped Peggy with her daycare children. Peggy adored my little sister and had a way of making all of the children in her care feel special.

Later, I discovered that Peggy's daughter Jennifer, Caitlin's middle school teacher, was there and had hoped I'd come along because she had a question for me. Jennifer pulled Mom aside and asked if she thought I'd be willing to speak to her students about being on Animal Planet.

Mom hesitated, remembering how hard it had been to just get me to go to Chuck E. Cheese's. "I don't know," she finally said, "but if you were to ask her instead of me, she'd be more apt to say yes."

After hearing Jennifer's request, I hemmed and hawed. Speaking at a middle school? The thought didn't thrill me. Even so, how could I let Caitlin's teacher down? This woman wasn't just an acquaintance. She was a family friend.

I agreed—with great reluctance.

My visit was a few weeks away, and already my stomach was in knots. What would the students think of me? I desperately wanted to get out of going, but something held me back. Before I knew it, the day had arrived. I was due at Caitlin's school in half an hour.

When I began trembling, Mom noticed and asked me what was wrong.

I told her, "I can't go back into a school full of eighth graders. The elementary school was one thing, but middle school is another! The memories keep flashing through my head. I feel sick! I keep seeing myself walking down the eighth grade halls. The students are making fun of me. I can't bear to have it happen all over again. I have no way of knowing if these students will treat me the same way!"

Mom interrupted me. "Gabe, you're not going alone. I'm going to be with you."

I barely heard her. All I could think of was the middle schoolers laughing at me and throwing spit wads and everything else they could get their hands on. My frazzled mind was made up. I was not going.

I asked Mom to call Jennifer and cancel.

Mom looked at me, "Did *I* say I would bring my dog to the school and share what it was like being on Animal Planet?"

"No."

"Who did?"

Crying, I admitted, "I did."

"Then, you better do the calling," She replied.

I knew Mom was hoping I wouldn't, but I had every intention of canceling, so I started dialing the number as I reiterated, "I don't want to go into schools, Mom!" I was about to push the last number when her words stopped me.

"Gabe, think about this! You're due to be at the school in a half hour. If you don't go, the kids are going to be disappointed. They don't care about your disease. They just think it's pretty cool that you and Izzy were on Animal Planet."

"Gabe," she added, "if you confront your fears, they'll go away."

After a long pause, I said, "Okay, stop! I'll do it, but I have three requests."

With no show of expression, Mom said, "Okay, let me hear them."

"First, I don't want to go in the front door of the school."

"No problem."

"Second, I don't want to be seen in the hallways between classes."

"No problem."

"Third, I don't want any students asking me about my disease."

"No problem."

Mom's willingness to talk with Jennifer and make sure my requests would be carried out was the real clincher. I know I wasn't making this easy, but it was the best I could do.

She knew I would not want to use my wheelchair around my sister's friends, so she agreed that we would leave it at home. We were in a bit of a rush, so she put Izzy in the car and piggy-backed me to the car. In truth, it was easier for her this way. I was usually wobbly when she walked while trying to hold me up, but she never complained. She always said, "It's all right, I am happy to help you as long as you're trying to help yourself."

As we drove toward the school, I was visibly shaking. Fortunately, we only lived a mile from the school, but I was still uneasy. Mom must have known I would be because she had our wonderfully supportive friend Linda meet us there. Once out of the car, my legs began to tremble and my voice quivered so much I was sure the kids would notice. As long as they didn't laugh at me, I'd be all right.

It was difficult getting into the school, but mom held me tightly, never letting go. My balance was off, but with Mom's help, I made it. She smiled my way, and I knew what she was thinking: as hard as this was, it would be good for me.

Linda held Izzy's leash and she trailed a short distance behind us.

When we finally arrived at the classroom, Mom knocked at the door. Jennifer was there to greet us, and as I stepped over the threshold, my body trembled as badly as my legs.

The students immediately called out to Izzy, and, boy, was I relieved. I could handle this with ease if it were all about Izzy.

Mom had been right. They were all thrilled to meet my dog. As soon as Linda let go of the leash, Izzy didn't lie down as usual. Instead, she walked through the aisles, visiting with the students who were laughing in delight. The students petted her as she walked by them. Izzy definitely had a mind of her own that day. Maybe she knew her antics would put my mind at ease. Either that or she smelled food and was determined to look for it.

We did have a wonderful time eating pizza, drinking pop, and munching on popcorn. Soon afterwards, the students asked questions about Izzy and me being on Animal Planet. They wanted to know all about the rock she

---

LETTERS OF APPRECIATION

I always look forward to getting home to read the many letters from students and adults we've met along the way. Here are just a few:

—*I want to thank you for coming to Durand Middle School! I have changed and inspired many of my friends and I saw many of the girls who were so sad for you that they started to cry. You've changed my mind about a lot of things about bullying. I used to bully a few other students and call them names. I wish you and Izzy a happy life together and I thank you for inspiring me.*

—*Hi! I just wanted to tell you thank you for coming to our school. I thought you really changed everything around and made my day because when my class left the gym and got back to the classroom, they all said they were sorry for all of the pain they have caused me by calling me names.*

ingested and what kind of dog she was, and they asked about her liver shunt. That day Izzy was the star, not me, and that was perfect.

The whole experience was nothing like I envisioned. The entire class was nice, and I had a good time. One of the boys drew a nice picture of Izzy and gave it to me before we left the classroom. I was pleasantly surprised.

The National Ataxia Foundation Association (NAFA) called and asked Mom if we were coming to the convention that year. We hadn't planned to, but that all changed when they asked Mom if she and I would be willing to speak about our experience on Animal Planet and how Izzy's disease had helped me to cope with my FA.

Mom was asked to address the adults, and I was supposed to speak to teenagers with FA. As it turned out, this was yet another step toward building my confidence.

The San Diego convention was close to where my Aunt Mary Lou was living at the time. Plus, it would be an opportunity to visit my friend Sean who lives in Santa Barbara. Sean wrote to Animal Planet after seeing my segment and the network forwarded the letter to me. We have been great friends ever since. Thoughts of seeing Sean and my aunt were two more reasons I agreed to speak at the convention.

Mom mentioned our upcoming trip to the convention while on the phone with Uncle Clayton. Although I was well versed in the subject matter, my experience in public speaking was greatly lacking. His desire to give me more experience before the event prompted his invitation to come and share my story with his scholarship class in Flint. He'd seen the Animal Planet episode and wanted me to share with his class what it was like being bullied. I reluctantly agreed to do it, having no idea how hard it would really be. As the day approached, I pondered what I would say, but nothing really came to me.

My mind, though anxious, eased when my sisters agreed to come and bring their dogs Dominik and Lindsay Belle. Since the topic I was supposed to cover was difficult for me, I convinced myself that having the dogs along would take some of the attention off of me. As it turned out, I was wrong, but not knowing it at the time was a comfort.

Izzy and I waited in the hallway alone until Uncle Clayton was ready to introduce us. I was nervous. I rarely talked to anyone in great detail about the bullying I had endured. I was ashamed and embarrassed by the way I was treated, so the thought of sharing this with a group of strangers was very uncomfortable. Unfortunately, it was too late to back out. I entered with Izzy at my side. As I shared my experiences with bullying, I began to cry, but I continued in spite of my tears.

In the days that followed, I received several comments in my online guestbook, thanking me for taking the time to come, visit and share my personal experience. The students not only said they would never forget me, but also that they were truly inspired.

My uncle was right. The experience did me a world of good. By the time I reached the NAFA Convention, I was better prepared. The teenagers I addressed at the convention enjoyed hearing about Animal Planet. Most of the attendees had a disease similar to mine and when I discussed how I had been bullied in school, many were able to relate. To have the opportunity to share Izzy's story was equally important. After all, it was Izzy's adoption and my caring for her with her own rare disease that helped me look beyond my own pain and loneliness. Izzy had given me a reason to live again.

Later at the convention, Mom encountered yet another blessing, this time in Bart Ferris. He had mentioned to Rick, my stepfather, that he'd seen me on Animal Planet. Rick called Mom and me over to introduce us.

During our conversation, Mom mentioned that she had a sister who lived in upstate New York. She commented on how beautiful she found the state. Soon enough, Bart mentioned an apartment in Manhattan that he owned but wasn't living in full-time. He planned to put it on the market in June but offered its use to us if we wanted to visit the city sometime soon. Mom immediately jumped at the idea. They exchanged phone numbers when Mom took a chance and asked Bart, "Would it be all right if Gabe and I make this a girls' trip? I'd like to bring along my other daughter Caitlin, Gabe's Aunt Linda, her cousin Tracy, and her Aunt Joanne."

He grinned as he said, "No problem, but no more!"

When Mom started laughing, so did he.

Mom had a one-track mind after that. She couldn't wait to get home and start planning the girls' trip to the Big Apple.

Our story continued to spread. The Muscular Dystrophy Association's *Quest Magazine* called to do an article on Izzy and me in their August 2004 issue. We had been in two AKC dog magazines but never a human health magazine. We were excited and hoped to be an inspiration to others. I was even more surprised when we learned that Izzy and I would be on the front cover of the magazine, especially after we found out that the same issue would carry an interview with Larry King.

The *Quest* article led to an engagement at Ore Creek Middle School in Hartland, Michigan, after my mom's friend Sharon showed the article to the principal. This time I spoke in an auditorium, not a classroom. The space was filled to capacity with the entire seventh and eighth grade classes. The students were especially quiet, and all eyes were riveted on me. I had their complete attention. Were they really listening? It appeared so. None of them made a disturbance of any kind. This was an opportunity that few, if any, would ever get with these students. If only I could help them understand bullying's long-term impact and how important it is to be accepting of other's differences.

Amazingly, I didn't panic. When I finished speaking that day, I realized I was finally winning the battle over my fears. I was enjoying myself, and, in the process, lives were being changed.

Before I knew it, the assembly was over. Afterwards, many students came forward to hug me, some of them shook my hand, and others came to pet Izzy. Many told me how much my visit had meant to them. As the students left the auditorium that day, my heart was warmed by the enormity of what had just taken place. These students were strangers, yet, because I had been willing to share my painful experiences, their eyes were being opened.

Kids were putting themselves in my shoes and learning about empathy. I was taken aback.

Not long after we returned home from the convention, other teachers began calling our home, each asking me to come for a visit. Kids love dog stories, and ours was not only unique—it was a bit mysterious as well.

Every time I stood before a group to speak, it became easier. My anxieties lessened. I realized I was enjoying myself, and it became obvious that those in the audience were glad I came.

At times, tears would come to the eyes of those listening and I would wonder, *"Are they crying because of the impact bullying has had on me or them? Or are they the ones who have bullied and are regretting the wrongs they have imposed on others?"* Whatever the reason, one thing was certain: lives were being impacted. Students and educators were now aware of the long-term effect bullying can have on a person.

 Many visits impacted me as much as they did the students. I spoke at my old elementary school, Tomek Eastern. Madeline wheeled me down the long hallway on that day and wonderful memories flooded my mind. I had run so freely through those hallways as a child (when the teachers weren't looking, anyway). However, those years had been my dancing years. Remembering how my life and my dreams had changed so dramatically made those memories bittersweet.

As I spoke more, I dug deeper into my experiences. My stepsister Lisa, now a high school English teacher, was covering bullying in one of her classes and her students had prepared a list of questions for me. My heart sank. High school kids had a tendency to inquire into more personal subjects, and it wasn't long before tears would be trailing down my cheeks. Deep, painful memories would be resurrected.

I had become an expert at hiding my feelings after years of being bullied on a daily basis, but how could I help these kids if I weren't willing to be honest? My old motto—if I don't talk about it, I won't have to deal with the pain—had to go. I could only hope that, like speaking in front of others, digging through my painful past would get easier, too.

After the event, I ran into one of Lisa's coworkers. She shared with me how much my story had helped one of her students. All the pain I had experienced that day was suddenly worth it all.

At other times, I was revisited by my old public speaking fears. One time, my mom's cousin Debbie Owens in Indiana, a teacher, asked me to speak at her school. We were happy to go. This school was located in Papa's hometown, where many of my relatives owned businesses and lived.

But during the first assembly, my old fear welled up inside me. For one of the longest minutes of my life, I lost my train of thought. I couldn't relax enough to get it back. I panicked. Caitlin, sensing my uneasiness, approached me to help me recapture my thoughts. Mom stayed on the sidelines. It wasn't like her not to come to my rescue. She always had before. She told me she remained silent for one reason alone: if I were to continue with public speaking, she wanted me to learn how to get back on course without her.

I was embarrassed to have lost it with so many of my relatives present, but it was too late for regrets. I wondered, *"Did I let them down?"* Mom assured me that I had not and that I was worrying for nothing.

After the sessions, my family ate dinner together at one of the local lodges. I'm convinced that half the town was there. I was shocked and happy. Everyone was warm and kind, and it was great to see my family and friends again. I had almost forgotten what a wonderful and supportive family we have.

By the time I came home from Indiana, I had an intriguing request from Linden Middle School. Instead of talking about my disease, they wanted me to speak at their Career Day. They asked me to encourage the students to reach for the stars by getting focused on life after high school. I was to address an assembly of eight hundred middle school students. Izzy and I would be alone in front of all of them.

I knew I could do it. My confidence was building with every assembly. I was pushing myself harder and facing my anxieties head on.

There was so much I could tell them; I decided to speak from my heart. It didn't take long to gain their undivided attention. I filled them in on how difficult my school days were. I even shared the challenges of traveling in a wheelchair. And then I told them that if I could graduate with my limitations, they could too! They could reach their dreams if they believe in themselves.

During the question and answer time, one young boy stood up and said that my presentation was the best his school had ever had. Suddenly, he wasn't standing alone; the other seven hundred ninety-nine students stood up with him! Receiving a standing ovation from eight hundred students was something I will never forget. It was truly awesome, not because I was looking for praise, but because these were middle school students—the ones I had feared the most.

I had come far. This experience changed me on the inside. If I could get through to eight hundred middle school students, maybe I was, in fact, fulfilling my purpose in life.

Over time, schools from all across the country requested me to come speak, all through word of mouth. There were so many requests, our Web site added a place for schools and groups to book engagements. While we enjoy traveling, it can be exhausting for both my mom and me. With my physical limitations, the brunt of the work falls on Mom. I worry about her pushing too hard, but whenever possible, Caitlin, Madeline, and Rick come along to help share the load.

I have great fun traveling with my Izzy girl. She creates quite a stir, especially at the airport. Izzy moved slowly and fatigued easily at this time. She rode to her gate in an oversized wheelchair or a special wagon as her disease progressed. As you can imagine, this was not a sight many passersby had seen before. Izzy didn't seem to mind the whispers, stares, pointing and good-natured laughter. She loves the attention and, on occasion, says so with her one-of-a-kind coondog howls.

I remember one of our flights from New Mexico a man with a wonderful sense of humor who knew us from previous trips took it upon himself to push Izzy all the way to our gate. As if Izzy were a celebrity, he'd look pilots, flight attendants, and passengers right in the eye and announce in his resounding voice, "Say hello to Izzy! Say hello to Izzy!" And they did.

Once on one of our longer rides to a gate, Izzy decided to sit up in her wheelchair, and her long black tail flowed out the back of her seat. We cracked up, and so did those who stopped to gawk.

I now can see clearly all I would have missed had I allowed my fears to keep me bound—had I turned down this chance of a lifetime. While every new step in my journey is not without its challenges, I now face them with the realization that fear is not my friend.

If someone would have asked me several years back what I would be doing with my life after high school, not in my wildest dreams could I have imagined that I would be speaking out in public about anything—least of all bullying. I found that I am still dancing. I am on a new stage dancing a different dance, making the world a better place—one school at a time.

CHAPTER EIGHT

New York Ladies' Trip

To turn down Bart Ferris's generous offer to allow us to use his New York City apartment free of charge was unthinkable.

Our trip to San Diego had severely taxed our financial resources, but that only forced us to get creative. Mom and Aunt Linda came up with a plan to take "ladies' week out" from dreamland to reality. We needed money—lots of money—so we organized garage sales to get our traveling pool started. Aunt Linda took those funds (and our other contributions) and tightly budgeted the trip. She has a tendency to be overly detailed so we voted her in charge of expenses. She had a separate fund for everything: one for gas, tolls, taxis, buses, food, even one for the miscellaneous items the group deemed necessities along the way. She had one goal for us, besides having fun: She wanted us to make it to New York and then have enough left over to get back home when it was all over.

Before we knew it, the big travel day arrived. Mom's 2000 Toyota Sienna was packed with suitcases and people. Mom sat in the driver's seat, with me beside her and Caitlin and Aunt Joanne behind us. We still needed to pick up Aunt Linda and my cousin Tracy and all their luggage in Shortsville, New York (about an hour from Buffalo).

We arrived at Aunt Linda's after almost seven hours of driving. Her home was a welcome stop for a vanload of weary travelers. She had dinner waiting for us as usual. Her home always had a welcoming glow. As we entered, the irresistible scent of Yankee candles mixed with the aroma of her scrumptious soup simmering on the back of the stove. It was a comfort.

We fell into bed early that evening and were back on the road early the next morning with our two new passengers, Aunt Linda and Tracy. While I'm not sure how she did it, Mom managed to stuff their luggage in as well. There were six suitcases, six women and one wheelchair. As you can imagine, the wheels on the van sat low with the load.

Our plan was to get into the city, take a short tour, and then reach Bart's home early that evening. The plan went well until we approached the Holland Tunnel. Mom had a phobia regarding tunnels—especially tunnels that go underwater. As we approached the tunnel, Mom's complexion paled, and she kept saying that her hands were sweaty. We gave her a pep talk—even reminded her that it was the fastest way into the city—but she wouldn't buy it. We finally convinced her that there were no other options. Another route would take too much time and make a short tour of the city impossible. Still, we were at her mercy—and all of us knew it.

When we finally talked her into proceeding through the tunnel, we silenced the giggles bubbling up inside. Mom was obviously nervous. She did her best to avoid hitting the sidewalls. While we kept our observations to ourselves, the way she crept along with other cars flying by us seemed simply hilarious.

Finally, we couldn't keep our silence any longer. Tracy sheepishly murmured, "I hear water, but don't tell Aunt Rhonda." It was too much. Unable to contain ourselves any longer, we all burst into laughter. Fortunately, it helped Mom relax—if only slightly.

Our short van tour wasn't so short. We took in Battery Park, Ground Zero and other sites. It didn't seem to matter how often we had already visited the city, it had the same impact on us.

Before realizing how late it was getting, darkness settled in, stealing the light and our ability to see where we were headed. Soon the handwritten directions to Bart's apartment that had appeared to be so simple and straightforward now looked like a treasure map against the backdrop of the big city. We took a wrong turn and drove from a very affluent area to a darker, rougher one. Someone hit the door lock and several of us jumped. I was just beginning to relax again when Mom asked us to pray for green lights, so we wouldn't have to stop. My muscles tensed. Although I did whisper a prayer, I kept my eyes peeled—for what, I did not know.

Aunt Linda suddenly recognized our surroundings. "We're in one of the worst parts of the city, Rhonda!" Her words held no comfort. Out of desperation, Aunt Linda grabbed the cell phone and called Bart. After a few minutes, we were back on track. The sweet laughter that filled our souls chased our fright away, but we did wonder if this was any indication of how the rest of our trip would pan out. We hoped not. Everyone was relieved to finally meet Bart at the apartment.

He introduced us to the doorman Andy, explaining that we were visiting and would be in and out of the apartment throughout the next several days. Andy realized I was in a wheelchair and went to the trouble of getting a removable ramp. Mom told Andy that it wasn't necessary. In fact, I remember her chuckling when she told him that she didn't have a doorman back in Michigan and she didn't want to get too spoiled while visiting Manhattan. Andy put the ramp away and let the girls handle me and the chair, since there were only three outside steps.

The Big Apple had little in common with our small hometown. Adjustments had to be made at every turn. Simple things we took for granted now had elaborate constraints and regulations, such as finding a parking space for the van. Space was limited, and it didn't take long to figure out that if we weren't in a parking space on the street by early evening, we would have to park in the huge garage that had strange similarities to a *tunnel*. Even which side of the street we parked on had regulations. Depending on the day, we'd have to park on one side of the street or the other—to accommodate street cleaners or garbage pick-up.

As if that weren't confusing enough, what in the world did the "No Standing" signs mean? Could we park in those spots or not? It was one of those peculiar things that made you feel silly to have to ask.

The first evening, we sat in Bart's apartment totally exhausted. We reviewed the highlights of our day when Tracy, who always had a Diet Coke in her hand—even when she was sleeping—took a sip, slipped off her shoes, and admitted, "My feet are killing me!"

Unable to resist, I added, "My feet are killing me, too!" Instantly, everyone in the room turned to look at me, and burst into laughter.

After a good night's rest and a quick breakfast, we were ready to hit the streets again. We started on Fifth Avenue for some serious window-shopping at stores such as Versace and Cartier. At Tiffany's, Caitlin, Mom and I made our way up the elevator with Aunt Joanne to take a gander at the necklace displays. Of course, Caitlin found one she had to try on, but when the price tag surpassed her Uncle Ray's Dairy Land paycheck, she put it back.

Aunt Joanne leaned over and whispered in my ear, "Looks like a dog collar if you ask me!"

I giggled and said, "It does. Izzy would look good in it, don't you think?"

From there, we visited China Town, SoHo, and the South Street Seaport (Pier 17), where the jugglers were out in rare form. Throughout the week we saw almost all the city's top sites. The Empire State Building was a must see, as was the New York Stock Exchange, Grand Central Station, Central Park, and the United Nations building. We traveled as much as we could by van, driving to a general area and walking (or wheeling) the rest. Mom always seemed to find a parking spot, no matter how tiny.

We went to Battery Park on several occasions. There was something special about being able to look out across the harbor at the Statue of Liberty. My mind filled with wonder as I considered all the immigrants who came through Ellis Island in hopes of starting a new life here in America.

While I found the mimes in the park intimidating—and somewhat frightening—Caitlin liked to push my chair there, finding pleasure in rolling me up to them. Although I would grab my wheels and try to stop her, she'd laugh when the mimes would put their arms around me for a photo.

Traveling by wheelchair had its challenges—even for resourceful women like us. After we'd park the car, we'd sometimes travel by cab to reach attractions. As tourists in a big city, we figured cabs would be a way to save time and not get lost. Aunt Linda and Mom would hail the cab but find that some cab trunks could accommodate a wheelchair and some could not. It was frustrating knowing that we couldn't depend on the cabs to get us where we wanted to go.

I had to keep a close eye on all the ladies in our group, especially Mom. They made a habit of hanging their packages on the back of my wheelchair. The added weight made it harder for me to push, but more important, I didn't want to forget they were there and repeat what happened the last time I was in New York. That time, I had gone to the ladies room at the American Kennel Club and, not thinking about the heavy packages, transferred out of my seat. To my astonishment, the chair flipped. It was not easy flipping it back over alone. The thoughts running through my head were anything but congenial!

"What were those dim-witted girls thinking? They loaded down my chair with their blasted bags!"

Across from Central Park, we went into the Plaza Hotel to take a gander and snap a few photos. we traveled to Trump Tower, where we shopped around for quite a while. The men working the elevators told Caitlin and me not to be surprised if we saw Donald Trump walking through because he was there filming *The Apprentice*. Unfortunately, we never saw The Donald.

Later that day, we saw where *The David Letterman Show* was filmed. We even strolled by Fox News, so we could tell Papa, who was an avid fan of Bill O'Reilly and Sean Hannity, that we were there.

One of New York's many free attractions is its people. We had lunch outside one day at a restaurant in Little Italy across from a place called Spring Lounge. We watched the hustle and bustle the city life brings when suddenly Aunt Joanne said, "Look, there goes Meg Ryan!"

It was thrilling to see a celebrity walking around right in front of us. While we did our best not to let our excitement show, it wasn't easy. While I do believe it's important to respect celebrities' privacy, I must admit, inside I sure did want to go over and say, "Hello."

We ate most of our evening meals at Carl's, a hamburger joint near Ground Zero. The atmosphere was inviting, and the corner street vendors added the type of hustle and bustle that could only be found in big-city life.

If asked, I'd have to say my favorite place to be in New York is Times Square. The larger-than-life buildings and the thousands of lights make me feel so small by comparison, and there's constantly something going on. I love everything about it. Seeing the diversity of people, many from other countries, leaves me in awe and wonder. Although some of our differences are on the surface and some are within, the similarities are exposed as well. I walked away feeling challenged to look beyond my own culture and investigate others.

Sightseeing in the city reminded us we had much for which to be thankful. Seeing the homeless sleeping on park benches in Battery Park awakened something inside of me—inside of all of us. There were so many in need.

We visited St. Paul's Chapel, where George Washington worshiped on his Inauguration Day, April 30, 1789, when New York was the country's capitol. After the attack on the World Trade Center Towers, the chapel was a place of refuge for the recovery workers. Today, the chapel contains an array of artifacts from the 9/11 tragedies. My body felt numb as I realized how many of the workers at the museum had lost family members in those senseless attacks.

We visited Ground Zero several times. The structural damage to buildings from the impact of the explosion was plain to see. Visiting the actual site and seeing the many letters and flowers still posted from loved ones brought it all back. Caitlin and I glanced over and saw a firefighter leaning up against the garage doorframe of Fire Station Ten. We headed that way and struck up a conversation with him. We talked for a while about the tragedy before going in to buy T-shirts with "Engine One" and the station number on the sleeve. We wear the T-shirts faithfully every year on 9/11 in memory of those who lost their lives.

Mom bought a "Flag of Honor" for her friend Barb, who knew someone who lost her life in one of the planes that hit the towers. It contains the names of all those who lost their lives at the World Trade Center, at the Pentagon, and on all four of the flights that day.

A feeling of dread washed over me as I looked at the hole where the towers once stood so tall. The ceremonies we attend every year as a family help us to remember what happened and to be thankful for our blessings.

Each evening we returned to Bart's apartment with our many packages. Walking through the lobby, we would stick our noses in the air and tell Andy, "We're new money!" (Like the unsinkable Molly Brown who survived the Titanic tragedy.) He'd start to laugh and have a horrible time regaining his composure.

During our stay, we learned that while Bart spent most of his time at his home in the Catskills, he raised his family in this extravagant apartment. The beautiful winding staircase led to many spacious bedrooms, all of which had fireplaces, giving the rooms a welcoming appeal. What a place to grow up! Bart, out of concern, asked Mom how I went up and down the stairs at night. He was surprised to find out that I crawled. Since he, too, had been diagnosed with a type of late onset ataxia, I believe he was also curious as to what the future could look like for him.

In the evenings, we would usually find him watching the NBA basketball playoffs between the Los Angeles Lakers and the Detroit Pistons. Aunt Linda, who had a son who played sports, was as enthralled by the games as Bart, so he'd gladly fill her in on anything she missed.

Bart amazed all of us. He never seemed to mind the interruptions of our presence in his life during our stay. That we could get around the city as well as we did and take in so many sites astounded him. Every evening before we would call it a night, he'd ask us where we were heading the next day. He truly wanted to know. There aren't many people who would reach out to others the way he had. Our lives truly have been richer for knowing him—and I have a sneaking suspicion that goes both ways. To this day, we have stayed in touch.

Every day when we returned to the apartment Andy was there to greet us, always excited to hear about our daily adventures. Throughout the week we got to know the doorman, Andy on a personal level. A native of Eastern Europe, he told us often how impressed he was with our self-reliance. We handled our own suitcases, the wheelchair, and other items without asking for his assistance, and he said this was definitely not the norm. He enjoyed hearing about our daily adventures, but it was clear from his reactions that he was unaccustomed to being around such resourceful women. He still couldn't believe six women could do so much in one day, especially while having to maneuver me in my wheelchair. We told him Mom always found a way, wheelchair accessible or not. She refused to let a tricky path hinder us from getting where we wanted to go. Her desire to help me explore life to the fullest kept me going even when things got difficult.

Andy loved our story about the man who helped me while I was on the Hudson River Harbor Cruise. I wanted to sit with the other girls on the top of the boat where we were sure to get a great view of the skyline, but there was no way to get my chair up to the top deck. Mom tried to help me walk up the stairs, when a helpful man offered to carry me up to the top deck. We thanked him repeatedly, but he assured us that he was pleased that he could lend a hand.

Mom explained to Andy: "While we don't often hear about their kind deeds, there are countless citizens in the world willing to lend a hand to those in need." Andy was clearly moved by our story, and we knew without asking that he wouldn't have thought twice about helping in the same way if he were near.

Not everyone we encountered was so selfless. A woman who lived in the apartment building drove up to the front entrance of the building in her sleek, black BMW. She got out of her car, opened her trunk, and pulled out a little brown paper bag, the size of a school lunch sack. In the bag was an apple. She placed the bag on the red carpet and directed Andy to take it up to her apartment while she parked her car.

We were flabbergasted. After the lady left to park her car, Mom shared a thought or two with Andy. While her thoughts left him in stitches, he was well aware that his opinion in the workplace was irrelevant. His job required him to have a servant's heart, and he did. Day after day he reached out to others and gave of himself no matter the cost. In the time we spent with this man, he had definitely captured our hearts.

On our last day in New York, we put our heads together and agreed that the perfect souvenir for each of us would be a new purse. Aunt Linda had already set the money aside to get home. As long as the trip home was uneventful, we were covered. After doing the math, we divided up the balance left in our pool and went shopping.

Although we were sad to leave the Big Apple, we had so many wonderful adventures to remember. How could we ever thank Bart enough for his extravagant act of generosity? Without it, we could not have afforded this ladies' trip to New York City. He will forever hold a special place in our hearts and minds.

We did make it home safe and sound and had managed to laugh most of the way. We had no way of knowing at the time, but this would be our last trip with Aunt Joanne.

CHAPTER NINE

Two of a Kind

The annual Fourth of July Parade in Fenton was always a cheerful event, and this year, my entire family planned to go. Since the walk was a bit much for Papa and me, Rick drove us into town while Mom, Caitlin, and Madeline walked with Izzy. Our plan was to meet on the corner.

While Izzy has always moved slowly and has never been very energetic, we were pretty sure she could make the trip—it was only four short blocks. I should have put her in her wagon, but I thought she could make it. She did, but as she moved up the walk toward me, I noticed how badly she lagged behind my mom and sisters. She looked exhausted. When Izzy lay down and didn't move much throughout the noisy parade, I was confused, but my confusion quickly turned to concern when she didn't even budge while the fire trucks blew their horns. When the parade came to an end, I tugged on her leash to let her know it was time to go, but her response was minimal.

An elderly man bent over to pat her head and said, "Poor ol' dog!" Curious he asked, "How old is she?"

When I told him she was only four, I don't think he believed me. To me, Izzy looked great! She had walked farther than normal that day, and it was hot, so I thought maybe she just needed some extra water.

I listened as others commented on my dog. They were saying things like, "Beautiful ol' hound dog!"

"She's not old!" My thoughts exclaimed in defense. *"She's only four! Yes, she has a liver shunt, but she's doing well, much better than her vets expected."* Feeling overly protective at the time, I mentally justified Izzy's odd movements. However, I really began to worry when Mom admitted, "She does seem to be struggling with the short walk, Gabe. Maybe you should take her to see Dr. Smith and have her liver checked. I hope she's fine, but things could be getting worse. It's a miracle she has done as well as she has." A sick feeling welled up in my stomach.

I made the appointment but Mom let me off the hook for the visit itself. I had been up all night, sick with worry, and my stomach was too upset to go anywhere. Mom thought it would be best if I stayed home.

Although Mom tried to assure me that Izzy would be okay, I wasn't so sure. I felt as though I was neglecting Izzy. After all, she was my furry little girl. I loved her, and as I watched them leave, I felt guilty, as if I were letting her down somehow. After all, I was supposed to be her caretaker, not Mom.

My bond with Izzy was special. The love we had for each other came without conditions. We had been there for each other through many lonely moments. I could tell her all my secrets like girlfriends do. Perhaps some would find this silly, but Izzy never laughs at me. She accepts and loves me no matter what I'm going through. Not being there for her when she was struggling made me feel empty, but I had to let it go. I was physically ill. Mom didn't need two sick patients on her hands.

When she returned, I was not surprised to learn that Dr. Anderson, an associate at Dr. Smith's office, was concerned about Izzy. She saw things I didn't: muscle atrophy in Izzy's back legs and her unsteady gait. I had noticed how slowly she walked, but her gait didn't seem unsteady or wobbly to me. Then, I wondered, *"Am I too close to Izzy to notice the changes, like Mom was with me?"* Dr. Anderson kept her suspicions to herself. She needed to run a liver test before she said more, so Mom sat with Izzy and waited patiently for the results. If only I could have been so calm while waiting at home.

The tests results finally came back. Dr. Anderson told mom that Izzy's liver was functioning better than it had when she was diagnosed with a liver shunt.

When Mom got home and told me this, I said, "Wow, that's great!" I was relieved, and Mom was, too—about that, anyway. I thought, *I was right. Izzy was just overheated the day of the parade.*"

Unfortunately, Mom had more to say: "Dr. Anderson told me Izzy looks just like you, Gabe."

Hearing the hesitancy in Mom's voice, my eyes met hers. Izzy had just been given a good report, but what was Mom trying to say?

Mom added, "I laughed and told Dr. Anderson, 'Yes, Gabe and Izzy are both kind of floppy.'"

When I thought about it, I realized how right Mom was—Izzy was kind of floppy, and so was I!

Mom continued to tell me about her conversation. "Dr. Anderson's expression got real sober when she said, 'Rhonda, Izzy moves just like Gabe.'"

Mom understood what she was saying. She looked right at Dr. Anderson and said, "Don't tell me dogs get muscle disease! If they do, this will really throw Gabe for a loop!"

"I'm sorry Rhonda, it is very rare, but they do."

Mom's heart dropped in her chest. How could this be?

When Mom told me Dr. Anderson suspected Izzy had muscle disease, I couldn't believe it. I thought Izzy had a liver problem! I had never heard of dogs having muscle disease.

Could she die from this?

I began to panic! I felt helpless again, like I did when Izzy was first diagnosed with a liver shunt. I thought, *Why my dog?*"

Dr. Anderson put in a call to Dr. Diane Shelton, one of the leading veterinary neurologists in the nation. Since Dr. Anderson had trained under Dr. Shelton, she knew her well. After sharing our story with her, Dr. Shelton wanted Dr. Anderson to send Izzy for a muscle and nerve tissue biopsy. It was to be flown to her at the University of California, San Diego (UCSD) so she could diagnosis the problem.

Dr. Anderson called OVRS to set up an appointment for Izzy to see the surgeon, who would perform the biopsy. Dr. Shelton said that if I allowed Izzy to be the case study of the month, there would be no charge for her to diagnose the nerve and muscle tissue.

The day arrived for her test, so Mom and I loaded Izzy into the van and took her for the appointment.

I felt bad for Izzy. She just *couldn't* have muscle disease. The thought of her being cut again did not sit well with me either, but it was necessary, so I set my discomfort aside. Until we found out what was wrong, her symptoms couldn't be treated. Dr. Anderson and Dr. Smith had always been so wonderful with Izzy. I trusted their judgment.

After I kissed Izzy on the nose, we left her and got something to eat. When we returned, she was still in surgery. We waited for what seemed like forever when the door to the waiting room finally opened. Izzy was with one of the techs who held onto a harness that helped her to walk. She favored the leg on which they had performed the biopsy. Colored tape was wrapped around her leg, and a bandage covered her shoulder blade where a piece of nerve was removed.

Unfortunately, she needed to wear a lampshape-like collar to keep her from chewing on the bandage. I hated seeing her like this. When we got in the car, I told Mom, "This is it! She's not going to be cut on again." I couldn't wait to get Izzy home.

Izzy was exhausted from her ordeal, so I lay down on the floor next to her and did everything I could to make her comfortable. After removing the collar, I rubbed her droopy face and ran my fingers down her long ears.

Anxiously, we awaited the call from Dr. Anderson. The news was not good. Izzy had a rare type of progressive muscle disease. Dr. Shelton told us she was going to send the tissue to Duke University to see if they could name the disease. I never did inquire. In truth, I didn't want to know. The treatment would be the same no matter what. All I wanted was for Izzy to live.

Like my disease, there was no magical treatment or cure. The only recommendation was to give Izzy CoQ Enzyme for balance and Vitamin E for heart health. Ironically, that was the exact recommendation I was given for my FA.

For a short time, both of us took these religiously, but we have since stopped. I don't think it made a difference, and we both had difficulty swallowing the pills. No matter how I tried to disguise the pills in her food, she would always manage to find them and spit them out.

Dr. Anderson once told a reporter who was doing a story about us, "I've been a vet for a long time, but I've never seen anything like this before. Gabe and Izzy are so bonded."

She sure was right about that.

Not long after Dr. Shelton diagnosed Izzy, she called and asked if I'd be willing to do a show with her and UCSD neurologist Dr. Geoffrey Sheean, called *People And Pets: Common Diseases—Ataxia*. Of course, I said, "Sure!"

In truth, I thought it would be fun. I had been speaking in schools for some time, and Animal Planet had cured me of my fear of the camera and interviews, so why not?

When we arrived at UCSD, there was a parking spot Dr. Shelton had reserved for us with orange cones and a sign that read, "Reserved for Gabe and Izzy." We were delighted that she had gone out of her way to welcome us, but at the same time, it was us who were honored to finally meet the woman who had gone out of her way to help Izzy. Izzy and my story aired throughout most of California.

Although I had been speaking in schools for a while, and had been on TV several times with Izzy, at times fears would fill my mind. I still had concerns about being seen by former students and even started to regress. When my beloved Izzy became ill, I was once again forced out of our home to seek medical help for her. Her new diagnosis of muscular dystrophy bonded us even more. Time would tell how much being there for Izzy through her struggles—that so much mirrored my own—would help me heal.

While our diseases are not the same, the symptoms of Izzy's muscle disease are very similar to my neuro-muscular disease. I stumble, Izzy stumbles, and we both have muscle atrophy and weakness. Our gait and balance are wobbly. My voice is sometimes weak, and so is Izzy's bark. I have wheels (my wheelchair), and Izzy has wheels (her wagon). Izzy can walk only a short distance. She uses a ramp, and so do I. We both hate going to the doctors to be monitored. These similarities have caused us to lean on each other for support.

Our journey has been filled with many unusual coincidences that no one wants to try and explain, but I am not convinced they were coincidences at all. There is no doubt in my mind that Izzy and I were meant to be together. As we continue to share our story with students, educators, veterinarians, medical personnel, and all the people we meet, it is our hope that hearts will forever be changed and challenged to move forward, no matter what.

CHAPTER TEN

The Winds of Adversity

Autumn's extraordinary display of vibrant shades faded slowly as the northern temperatures fell, giving way to a winter wonderland in Fenton. The snow had begun to fly, coating our world in a fresh, white blanket of icy flakes. The view was breathtaking.

While most of the families in our hometown prepared for the coming holiday, my family struggled at every turn. You see, the winds of adversity had begun to blow, and as we would soon discover, they would blow harder and stronger than ever.

On December 6, 2004, the anniversary of my grandmother Mimma's diagnosis of terminal cancer, Rick had an appointment to have a colonoscopy. His last visit with Dr. Anthony Daros, our family physician, gave cause for concern.

I asked Mom how his test went as soon as they returned home, fully expecting her to say fine. I was not prepared for her answer.

"Rick has a cancerous tumor, Gabe."

"What?" I was still trying to process what Mom had said, when she added, "He has an appointment to meet with a surgeon. He's going to need surgery as soon as possible."

Four days after Rick's diagnosis, my sister Caitlin was in an automobile accident. Rick later told me about the crash scene. As they approached the car, all Mom and Rick could see were tail lights sticking out of a row of pines that had fallen on impact. Caitlin was nowhere to be seen among the onlookers. Mom flew out of the car in which she and Rick had arrived, screaming out her daughter's name again and again, "Caitlin! Caitlin!"

When no answer came, she headed toward the police car.

Caitlin wanted to get out of the sheriff's car and answer Mom's frantic cry, but the female officer wouldn't allow it. Because of the late hour, the officer had assumed that Caitlin had been drinking and driving. When Mom reached the police car, she could not believe how cold the officer was toward Caitlin. Her daughter was terrified, and the officer was treating her like a common criminal.

The officer's assumptions were unfounded. It turns out Caitlin was just trying to do a good deed. As she left her job at Uncle Ray's Dairyland Ice Cream Parlor she realized that one of her coworkers had forgotten her purse. She decided to drop it off on her way home. As she drove out of town, the four-lane road she was on suddenly narrowed to two lanes. She didn't see the warning signs. When the car hit the gravel, she lost control. Crossing over into oncoming cars, Caitlin turned the wheel and swerved into a ditch on the side of the road. Thinking she had hit the brakes, she accidentally pushed hard on the accelerator. The car flew back across the road and went airborne, flying into a row of pine trees. She was terribly shaken, but otherwise unharmed.

Mom helped explain the circumstances of the crash to the officer, as well as the fact that Caitlin was in a student work program and an employee of the Holly Police Department. The officer stepped aside and allowed the recovery activities to move forward.

Rick's cancer and now Caitlin's accident, all in the course of a week. Surely we'd had our fill of surprises.

Four days after Caitlin's accident, at 4 a.m., the phone rang. I heard the ring and wondered who would call at that hour, but I was too tired to find out. I went back to sleep. Rick answered the phone; my Uncle Steve was on the other end.

According to Mom, Steve was practically screaming, but he and Rick always clowned around about one thing or another. For him to call in the middle of the night was a bit strange, but she didn't think anything about it, until Rick turned to her and said, "Joanne killed herself."

Mom jumped out of bed, ran downstairs, and grabbed the phone on the kitchen wall next to my bedroom. She needed to talk to Uncle Steve herself. She thought, *"This couldn't be true!"*

But it was.

Mom told her brother she would be right over, to stay calm and hold on. Knowing I could hear their conversation through the open door, Mom entered my room. She paused for a moment before saying, "Aunt Joanne killed herself, Gabe."

Mom's words hit me hard. "No!" I exclaimed. "Not Aunt Joanne! I love her so much." Rick told Caitlin to stay on the phone with Uncle Steve until he and Mom arrived. Caitlin sat with me on my bed. Why would Aunt Joanne do this? We couldn't cry. We were in shock, but we tried to comfort each other as much as we could.

The drive across town to Uncle Steve and Aunt Joanne's house seemed longer than usual to Mom, but she was thankful the Fenton Police were at the house when they arrived. Uncle Steve said he'd talked to Joanne at work only five hours earlier. Everything seemed normal. When he arrived home, he went to bed, and Joanne was beside him. Later, my eleven-year-old cousin Emily woke in the middle of the night. She was restless and when she couldn't find her mom in her room, she and Uncle Steve searched the house. When they didn't find her, Uncle Steve thought that perhaps she couldn't sleep and drove to Tim Horton's for coffee. He opened the garage to see if her car was gone, and there was his wife, hanging from the rafters.

Mom called to say that Papa had arrived and was bringing Emily home to stay with our family. Steve needed to get her out of the house. Madeline and Emily are close, so Mom was hopeful their friendship would play a part in helping Emily to cope with the tragedy.

It seemed like forever before Mom and Rick came home; they had to wait for the medical examiners to pick up Aunt Joanne's body. As painful as it was, Mom had to call Aunt Joanne's sister Cathy. Before long, our house was filled with family and friends who had come to comfort each other during this time of loss.

I loved Aunt Joanne, and while I would miss her dearly, I could only imagine what Uncle Steve and Emily were going through. Our families had shared many wonderful times together. I've had them to look back on, but the deep wounds left by Aunt Joanne's death may never fully heal.

Although my family was surprised when I rolled to the front of those gathered at Aunt Joanne's funeral to speak, I knew I had to say something.

I told everyone about the time I rode back from the MDA Telethon with Uncle Steve and Aunt Joanne. Izzy lay beside me when I mentioned I had a sweet tooth. Uncle Steve pulled into Walgreens but it was Aunt Joanne who went in to buy me the Twix bar I craved. When she returned, she handed me a huge bag of Twix bars. That was just like Aunt Joanne, always giving more than anyone would ever ask for. She had a good heart.

Although I came to understand the driving force behind Aunt Joanne's feelings of hopelessness and her desperate act, I can see so clearly that nothing good has been accomplished by taking her life. During some of my long periods of depression, suicide would cross my mind, but I would never do it. I had to keep telling myself, *"Tomorrow is a new day, and things will get better."*

After a time, my sadness turned to anger. I was mad at Aunt Joanne for leaving the way she did. She had everything I ever wanted—a husband, a beautiful daughter, a house, and, most important, her health.

Didn't she know she could come to us and we would help her with anything?

For some time after Aunt Joanne's death, my sisters, Emily and I struggled with the dark and we slept in the same room. Even Mom would have Rick meet her in the driveway when she came home late at night. Caitlin to this day cannot go into a garage. If only we could erase this nightmare from our minds. Most likely it will be with us for the rest of our lives. I don't voice my opinion when the subject comes up. I just sit quietly—recalling the pain of that dreadful night.

Christmas Eve drew near, and, although we had always celebrated with Uncle Steve's family, Mom wasn't sure what to do.

As much as we wanted life to return to normal, no one felt much like celebrating or cooking. When Sandy, Mom's friend from Dr. John Cabell's office, called to tell us that VG's Grocery would be delivering our turkey dinner Christmas Eve, Mom got teary eyed. Her heart was overwhelmed by their thoughtfulness.

This was the push we needed to lay our uncertainty aside and reach out. Uncle Steve and Emily needed us to be there for them, and we all needed to find a way to accept our loss and go on. The dinner we shared was delicious, but knowing we would be expected to unwrap the gifts Aunt Joanne had shopped for and wrapped left us all feeling a little sad. As difficult as it was, we managed to find joy in our time together.

If there were ever a family with a reason to be downcast it was ours, but Mom would not allow it. She stayed positive—as if there were no other option. She hated nothing more than whining and reminded us when we fussed about our circumstances that there's a silver lining framing every dark cloud. It might be thin, ruffled, torn, or hiding, but if we look hard enough, it can be found.

Rick was scheduled to have the cancerous tumor removed two days after Christmas. Although we believed this would be a surgical cure, the biopsy revealed cancer cells in the lymph nodes. He was in the hospital for a week, and Mom stayed with him the entire time.

Even after Rick got out of the hospital, he and Mom were rarely home. The doctor's appointments consumed their time. Mom has been blessed with many genuine friends, and they were there for us throughout every storm. Her friend Barb organized meals to be brought to the house. Our hearts were overwhelmed. Their efforts gave Mom the time she needed to take care of Rick instead of worrying about meals. I don't know how we would have made it through without their loving support.

It was late January before Rick met with the oncologist to explore his options for further treatment. He was not only going to need chemotherapy and radiation, but more surgery. This meant many more doctors' appointments throughout the next eight months, and Mom was with him for every one.

Rick finished his last radiation treatment and was scheduled for his second surgery. Unfortunately, there were complications. Scar tissue from the radiation meant a third surgery would be required.

We did everything we could to keep his spirits up. Uncle Bob even surprised him one time and drove in from New York to see him at the hospital. One time when Mom and I were out of town driving to a speaking engagement, Rick ended up in the emergency room and mom drove sixteen hours home to be with him. He was thrilled to see her.

After the third surgery, Mom encouraged Rick to keep walking. She didn't want him to give up. She helped him stay as active as he needed to fight his cancer.

During that long, arduous year, I spent much time reminiscing about the students who had a chance to share in my story. Often, after a visit to a classroom, I'd receive a large envelope filled with letters and colorful pictures from the students. I saved them all. Looking back brought so many wonderful memories to my mind, filling me with joy.

I could see clearly how the message I shared had impacted these students. The letters were heartfelt, and it was as if the students were sending me a basket filled with the fruits of my efforts. Not only have I influenced their lives, but they have also influenced mine.

I thought about speaking and where I would go from there. Aunt Joanne's death and Rick's cancer had taken me by surprise, but reading through the letters students sent made me realize that no matter what, I had to go on and speak louder than ever. I had a voice and it was my responsibility to use it. No one should feel alone. No one should feel that others aren't willing to help.

The storms continued. Madeline started having dizzy spells. Her doctors had to rule out a brain tumor, so they ordered a CAT scan and blood work. She was diagnosed with vertigo, something she still deals with to this day. I was so relieved to learn it was not a brain tumor. She is my little buddy. I couldn't stand the thought of something being wrong with her.

Summer 2006 was coming to a close. Although our family normally attended an annual memorial on September 11, that year our plans were altered when we ended up in the emergency room with Papa.

Mom and I arrived at Emily's soccer game and saw Papa. He wasn't feeling well, so he told Mom that he was going home to rest. After the game, Mom dropped me off at the house and picked up Rick to do some shopping. While they were gone, I heard Papa in the kitchen downstairs making odd noises, but I didn't think too much of it. He was always puttering around with something.

When Mom and Rick returned, Papa was still in the kitchen. When Mom tried showing him a magazine she had picked up with me on the cover, he didn't say anything. He just reached for a cigarette. Standing up, Mom got a better view of Papa's face and realized something was drastically wrong. She was pretty sure that, because of the way his face was drooping, he'd had a stroke. Then, she realized he could not talk. She encouraged him to sit down and called 911.

As much as Mom wanted to be wrong, she was not. The doctors at the hospital did not give him much hope. In fact, they told Mom to call hospice. They would be surprised if he had six months to live. Although his recovery has been slow, he is still living with us and has resumed his handyman endeavors around the house. We've been blessed.

By 2007, Mom had more on her plate than any mom should handle. She cared for Rick, held a job, set up my speaking engagements, and went to the engagements with me. As if all that were not enough, Caitlin was in her senior year. Prom, homecoming, and other events were approaching, along with graduation.

Mom had few moments to herself. She was only one person. How she held up under this kind of pressure was a mystery to me. All she did was run, run, run. The things she loved to do had to be set aside. Her life was about helping others.

In August of that year, while we were on the road driving to another engagement, it dawned on Mom that she had been so busy taking care of everyone else, she hadn't scheduled her yearly mammogram. Having lost her own mother to cancer, she knew how important these exams were. She called Rick, and he made the appointment for her.

At the appointment several weeks later, I went along. I waited for a long time, but this was just a routine test, so I didn't worry.

When she came back, I asked her, "How did it go?"

"Not good, Gabe. Something showed up on the test, and they think it is cancer."

I couldn't believe it. "Are they sure, Mom?"

"Yes. They are quite sure."

All I could think about was Mimma, my grandmother. She had been such an integral part of our lives, and in fourteen short months, she had withered away to fifty pounds. She died a painful death, and I couldn't imagine losing Mom the same way. Mom had always gone out of her way to hold our family together through trying times. No matter the storm, she would hang onto the good, and somehow we would get through together. Now she was the one suffering.

The tables had turned. If we were going to get through this, I needed to do everything I could to take care of her. I told Mom I would be her rock. She could lean on me. I would go to every doctor's appointment with her, and, like Rick, I would be by her side. When she had a biopsy performed in Flint, Rick and I went with her. Though the room was small, the doctor allowed us to be present during the procedure. She has since told me how much she was affected by my efforts.

To help calm her while waiting on her test results, I decided to make a mix CD of inspirational music. I spent two days burning music while she was at work. Some were songs I knew she loved, and others were songs I thought would inspire her. I put the CD in a plastic case and created liner notes entitled "Rhonda Kay's Mix." The hardest part of the project for me was cutting the paper to fit inside the cover of the CD case. It was a real challenge, since I don't have the best coordination in my fingers. It meant a lot to her when I gave it to her and she listened to it right away.

Mom wanted to live. She kept saying that her work on this earth was far from done. She remained lighthearted and kept saying, "Gabe, we are on a mission with your bullying presentations. I know down deep I'll be okay. I have to be." I felt the same way.

At times, Mom would get teary-eyed, but she always found humor in all she was going through. She teased me, saying, "If I have to have a mastectomy, I'm getting implants as big as yours, Gabe!" (It was the family joke that I ended up with the largest chest.)

Mom was at work when the doctor's office called and told Rick she needed to have three more biopsies. I waited a few minutes and called Mom at work to see if the doctor's office had contacted her as well. It had. I asked her if she was okay. She tried to make light, but she couldn't fool me. Her voice was trembling. I knew she was close to tears. I told her, "Mom you know those Ds you've been wanting? Go ahead and get them!" We both laughed through our tears.

I had three out-of-town speaking engagements scheduled starting August 16. Although Mom hated to leave town in case the call came in about her biopsies, rescheduling would be difficult. She decided to go.

Mom knew how much I enjoyed speaking and would do everything she could to see that I continued. When we crossed Michigan's border into Indiana, Mom's cell phone rang.

She looked at the phone and glanced over at me. I knew it was Dr. Daros's office. His nurse Jackie was on the line. She had Mom's test results, but she did not want to give them to her on the phone. Jackie wanted Mom and Rick to come into the office that evening.

When Mom told her that we were on the road and wouldn't be able to do that, she asked, "Jackie, can you tell me I'm not going to die? I am on a mission with Gabe, and we have a lot of work left to do."

"Dr. Daros does not want to give you the results over the phone, Rhonda."

Mom assured Jackie, "If you can tell me I'm going to be okay, I can handle the news."

I could tell by Mom's voice she was now talking directly to Dr. Daros. He informed her that she did have breast cancer, but her prognosis was good. The cancer was in the early stages, and they believed surgery would cure her. Out of the four biopsies, one was cancerous. After watching her own mother die the way she did, and seeing Rick suffer, Mom was not willing to take any chances. She wanted both breasts removed.

Mom said she could not have surgery soon enough. Jackie scheduled her an appointment with Dr. Shannon Bongers, a surgeon at the Karmanos

Cancer Center in Detroit who specialized in breast cancer. Dr. Bongers talked to Mom about her options, but Mom had already decided what she was going to do. She wanted a surgical cure. Dr. Bongers was very supportive and, I think, pleased with her decision. Dr. Bongers then told Mom to set up an appointment with Dr. Meininger, a plastic surgeon to discuss her options regarding reconstruction. He got a good laugh about the "D" story and assured her that it was "No problem!"

Mom wasn't concerned about her appearance after having the double mastectomy; she wanted her life. I'm glad she felt that way. We needed her, too!

I did my best to be the cheerleader Mom had been for me. Whenever she would seem down, or in deep thought, I'd wheel close to her and tell her we needed to go for a walk. I did my best to keep her going. Usually, I could cheer her up, but sometimes she just had to get out of the house. Living only five blocks from downtown Fenton was helpful. Often we'd go to Tim Hortons and get an iced cappuccino. The fresh air had a way of chasing away her darkest moods.

Mom always does her best to find the good in every situation, so I wasn't surprised when she told me the good part of her cancer was that, for a change, our roles were reversed. I was taking care of her, instead of her taking care of me. She was right, but there was more to it than that. That's just what friends do—they reach out to one another without thought for themselves—and no doubt about it, Mom and I are the best of friends.

Mom's surgery was on a Wednesday. The stress and turmoil of the day was almost too much for her to bear. When I told her I wanted to stay with her that evening, she seemed relieved. The change in her voice and countenance was dramatic. Uncle Bob was bringing Aunt Linda out to be with Mom during surgery and help her around the house for a while after she got out of the hospital.

We were all excited when Caitlin came home to be with us during this time as well. Caitlin had always loved the ocean and warmer climates, so after graduation she moved to Florida. She made arrangements to stay with Rick's cousin Tina until she could get a job, enroll in school, and get situated. While the distance has made frequent visits impossible, Mom and Caitlin remained close and it was great to have her home.

To nobody's surprise, Mom wanted to leave the hospital the morning after her surgery. It felt like déjà vu. Mom's friend Laura organized meals every night for three weeks, so she wouldn't have to worry about cooking. This time, it wasn't about Mom needing time to be with Rick; it was about her needing time to heal.

Mom loved the idea that she had her three girls together. She planned to attend the Fenton Homecoming Parade and football game that weekend after her surgery. No one wanted to argue with her that day, so we went along with her idea, knowing we would have to see how she felt after the surgery. But Mom would not be denied the opportunity, and that weekend, we found ourselves at the parade and football game.

Later, when Mom went for her follow-up, Dr. Meininger was upset with her, and rightfully so. She told him she felt great, but he had told her to rest, and she hadn't done that.

Mom left the office that day in tears. She called her friend at work to tell her that the doctor had chewed her out. Sandy's response surprised Mom. "Good! You need to rest, Rhonda. You don't stop! You need to take care of yourself." As shocked as Mom was, she realized that they both had her best interests at heart. From then on, I noticed that she tried to take it easy when she'd get tired.

I had another speaking engagement booked at Ore Creek, in Hartland, Michigan. Mom wanted to follow Dr. Meininger's advice, but she had never missed one of my assemblies—this would be a first. She told me she just wasn't up to going. When Rick offered to take her place, I agreed. I wheeled my chair toward the back door to go down the ramp to the car and yelled out, "Bye, Mom! See you later. It won't be the same without you!"

As we backed out of the driveway I saw Mom coming out the side door. She had her red coat on and was waving us down. Jumping into the back seat of the car, she said, "I've never missed an assembly. I want to be there for you today, Gabe!"

We were so surprised to have her with us. I returned the favor by surprising her with a thank you in front of the entire school assembly.

Mom returned for her implant surgery six months later. Dr. Meininger told her she was not to lift anything, and she was to rest afterward. Looking straight into her eyes, he half-jokingly said, "We do understand each other, don't we, Rhonda? We've been through this once before."

Mom said, "Yes!" and they both laughed. Mom finally listened. She didn't go back to work until Dr. Meininger said she could.

For three years, the winds of adversity blew hard. We thought that my disease and Izzy's disease had made us strong, but we had so much more to learn about ourselves. Our deep family roots helped us withstand the blows of cancer, car accidents, a stroke and tragic loss. For my part, I learned that I could give back, and be the caregiver others had been for me. In turn, my Mom, Rick and Papa learned that someone else could take the reins for them, and give them the rest that they so sorely needed.

Those winds may have caused some worry and sleepless nights, but they never rattled our foundation. In fact, those gusts showed us all our capabilities. They helped us understand that no matter how long the storm raged we would always have hope. We would always be on the lookout for the rainbow on the rise.

"NO SCHOOL BULLYING!"
Gabe and Izzy Publishing

CHAPTER ELEVEN

The Dominator's Spirit

Scattered throughout the challenges of those years were the trials brought on by my FA. I still refused to use adaptive equipment on a daily basis. I used the wheelchair only rarely, such as for vacations or trips to Izzy's vet. Mom wanted me to use a walker, but I refused. I told her I'd rather crawl or scoot on my butt around the house than use one of those things. At my appointment with Dr. Michel Nigro, an MDA specialist in Canton, Michigan, he and his assistant Maggie tried to convince me that it was necessary. I told them no way!

I maintained that I would have to break a bone before I'd give in to any other adaptive equipment at home. I would fall sometimes and those falls would often send me to the emergency room. But my injuries were minimal: a cut lip, torn ligaments in my ankle, a broken nose. I did bruise myself, again and again, but I simply could not give in to adaptive equipment. To do that, I felt, would mean admitting defeat. I was still convinced that my disease would not progress. I would walk, run, and dance again. I believed I could beat my disease.

A few weeks after our visit at Dr. Nigro's, I sat in the kitchen when the UPS man knocked on the front door. I knew what was in the huge box he brought into the house, but I signed for it and waited for him to leave. Unfortunately, it was too heavy for me to lift. If I could have, I would have taken it to the basement or thrown it out.

Mom came in from work all smiles—until she walked into the dining room and saw the box. There was no doubt in my mind she knew what was inside, but it wasn't labeled, so she assumed I was clueless.

Looking up at her, I said, "I know what is in the box!"

Mom shook her head. "No you don't, Gabe!"

"Yes, I do Mom."

"No, Gabe, you don't! You just think you do."

I told her, "I want you to put the thing in the basement, or I will burn it!" She knew I meant it, so she did. And that is where it stayed. She didn't want to pressure me, but she knew we needed to be prepared.

On August 22, 2005 was like any other summer day. Mom and Rick were at work. Madeline, ten at the time, was upstairs on the computer playing and singing along to songs she loved. Madeline always shut the door thinking no one could hear her, but often the rest of us would sit in the living room and laugh at how adorable she was singing her heart out. Papa was downstairs in his apartment. I was sitting at the kitchen table. I had just finished putting on my make-up, and my stomach was growling. I decided to make an instant breakfast drink. I made my way around the kitchen by hanging onto the tall heavy table Mom and Rick had bought to help me get around the kitchen easily.

I had just poured the package of powder into my favorite Goofy mug when I lost my balance and started to fall backward. With my right hand, I tried to grab the sink and pull myself forward, but the sink was wet and slippery, so I lost my hold. When I hit the floor, my left arm was caught underneath my body.

Immediately my arm began to burn like it was on fire. The pain was so intense I could hardly catch my breath. My face pressed against the floor. When I called out to Madeline, the words were barely a whisper. Again and again I tried, knowing she couldn't hear me because she was singing along with the music on her computer.

I began to feel faint. I kept calling, but my voice was fading. Papa heard me from his apartment and came upstairs. One look and he knew I was seriously hurt. He recognized the signs. He had several plates, pins, and screws in his own body holding him together from injuries he had acquired as a builder.

Papa wanted to help me get up but I told him not to touch me. I was in excruciating pain. He yelled for Madeline. As soon as she saw me, she grabbed the phone to call Mom at work.

I was blacking out, but I could hear Madeline talking:

"Mom, Gabe wants you to come home."

Mom must have asked Madeline if I was hurt because I recall hearing her say, "Gabe fell."

Mom was used to me falling. I'd get hurt and usually get back up and go on. She didn't want to leave work unless this was a true emergency, so she had Madeline ask me, "Do you want Mom to call 911?" "No." But Mom heard me crying in the background. Somehow, she knew she had to come home.

"Gabe," Madeline said, "Mom will be right here."

Before Mom left the office, she called the Fenton Police and told them I had fallen and that I had a disease that caused me to fall. I might be okay, but she wanted them to send a paramedic to the house.

Mom called Rick and let him know what was going on. Rick was in the area, so he arrived before the paramedics. Rick got two pillows, one for under my head and one for under my knees, and carefully, he and Papa rolled me over.

Madeline was standing nearby holding the dogs, because they kept licking my face. I closed my eyes, and the next thing I remember, the paramedics were standing over me. They began to cut the sleeve off of my favorite Dominator shirt, a line of sportswear created by former Detroit Red Wing Dominik Hasek. The shirt meant a lot to me and I couldn't watch them cut it. Both

Caitlin and I love the Red Wings and Dominik Hasek. In fact, a few years after I adopted Izzy, Caitlin got a dog and named him Dominik. We call him the "Dominator," for Dominik's sports nickname. The shirt meant more to me, though, because Dominik asked me himself to help promote his clothing line, saying that there was a dominator in all of us. He said I represented the spirit of his line, that it was meant to inspire people to challenge themselves.

It wasn't long after the paramedics arrived that Mom ran into the house. She told me later that she had been praying the whole way home. She couldn't bring herself to look at my arm. My expression told her that I was in horrible pain.

After checking my vitals, the paramedics put my arm in a splint.

They were getting ready to wheel me out on the gurney when Caitlin drove up. Mom told her what happened, and Caitlin came to my side and let me know she was there for me. I glanced over at Madeline before they lifted me into the ambulance. She was scared. I was, too. They asked Mom to ride in the front. I wanted her in the back with me, but it was not allowed. As scared as I was, I tried not to let on. Rick, Caitlin, and Madeline followed closely behind us in the car.

The paramedic periodically checked the capillaries in my fingertips and my pulse, but I didn't know why. He must have realized he was scaring me by the look on my face. He took a moment, and explained to me that he was just making sure my heartbeat was okay.

I couldn't feel my fingers, and that worried me. I kept asking him if they were going to have to amputate my arm or if he thought I might lose some of my fingers. He said he was pretty sure I wouldn't lose any limbs. He said it was a particularly bad break. The hospital would have to assess it. His attempt to get an IV started failed, due to the problems with my veins. He warned me that it would be a bumpy ride, and he wasn't kidding.

We pulled into the trauma area, and I was taken care of immediately. Rick, Caitlin, and Madeline arrived a few minutes after us. It wasn't long before they sent me down for x-rays.

At our request, the hospital sent the digital films to Dr. Bruce Lawrence, an orthopedic surgeon our family had dealt with many times. I lay there waiting. When I looked up I saw Mom looking down at me on the gurney with tears welling in her eyes. I knew she was struggling, so I told her, "Don't feel sorry for me, I did it my way. I wasn't going down until I was taken down."

She ran her fingers over the cuts in my favorite Dominator shirt and said, "Just like Dominik Hasek says, 'There is a Dominator in all of us!' "

After looking at the x-rays, Dr. Lawrence scheduled surgery to reset and repair the crushed bone in my arm for the next morning. He told me I had also dislocated the bone in my elbow and damaged a nerve. He couldn't say for sure, but I might need to have surgery on my elbow at a later date.

The doctors wrapped my arm and told me I could stay overnight at the hospital or go home. Mom wanted me to come home, so she could help me in and out of the bathroom. We left, picked up my prescription, and went home.

I hated it, but Mom had to cut the rest of my Dominator shirt off me when I went to bed. She couldn't get it over my broken arm. The temporary cast was so huge; it made my frail arm look like it belonged to the Hulk.

Although Mom lay down with me, neither of us slept. I was in pain and didn't want to be alone, so we just talked and rested as much as we could.

The next morning, Rick and Mom drove me to the hospital. The woman who came in to start my IV had a hard time with my veins just like the paramedic. It took a while, but unlike the paramedic, she succeeded. Once the IV was started, she gave me my medications, and I began to feel more at ease. The surgery went well, and I was admitted to a room for the night. I learned after surgery that it took a permanent plate and six screws to repair my broken arm.

Amanda, my dear friend, came with her grandma to bring me flowers. They definitely lifted my spirits. Mom's friend Davette was a nurse at the hospital. She was working that night, so she came in often to check on me. For one of her visits, she brought in a picture she had drawn of Izzy. Barb, a close family friend, visited later in the evening. I was medicated and don't remember all the kind ways people reached out to me, but I am thankful all the same.

Mom spent the night with me, but I'm sure she expected that we'd get a little more sleep than we did. I was restless, but I wasn't sure why—until I began to itch all over. Something was terribly wrong. As it turned out, I was having an allergic reaction to the medications. Hives covered my entire body.

Poor Mom was up most of the night with me again. Due to my broken arm, the task of scratching my every itch fell on her. Fortunately, the Benadryl kicked in after a while, and we were able to rest.

Unfortunately, morning came too soon that day with very little sleep from the night before. My family doctor entered my room, followed by Dr. Lawrence. I was released to go home. Mom could hardly wait to get me out of the hospital. She preferred taking care of me in our own comfortable surroundings.

I was afraid of getting addicted to codeine, so I took it only when it was absolutely necessary. I suffered as a result. I remember calling Mom into my bedroom many times asking her if the pain would ever go away. I began to wonder if my arm would ever feel normal again. Healing was slow, but eventually I was up and about. Mom refused to let me relapse into my old days of hiding away. My arm may not work, but my voice could. I had speaking engagements coming up at all three elementary schools in Fenton and one scheduled again in Hartland. I had to re-schedule only one of the elementary schools. I was determined not to let my arm be the end of my speaking career. With my arm in a cast, I continued to speak.

CHAPTER TWELVE

It's My Party and I'll Bark If I Want To!

Izabel was born on New Year's Eve in 1999. With her health condition, every day with her was a gift. As her eighth birthday approached, an idea brewed in my mind. I wanted to honor her with a birthday party that would show others just how much she meant to me—a very special party.

Every New Year's Eve since her arrival, the festivities in our home have included a birthday party for my little girl. To some this might seem strange, but not to me. When I consider the profound effect Izzy has had on my life, how could I not honor her? Dominik and Lindsay Belle (my sister's dogs) have always attended our annual party, complete with party hats, cake, ice cream, and gifts—something that only a dog would love. This year she would be eight, an age I never thought she would reach. So, I wanted this party to be extra special.

Izzy's story had touched more lives than just mine. She had even achieved celebrity status—a certain porter heralds her name through the corridors of the local airport. A mere "party" was not good enough this year. This year we were going to have an all out *celebration!*

With the help of our friend Laura, we managed to get everything organized and underway. The party was to serve as a two-fold commemoration. First and foremost, we would celebrate Izzy's eighth birthday. Second, I would celebrate signing the contract to have my memoir published. I knew without a doubt that this would be a great day!

After our initial planning, I couldn't wait to begin working on the many details. I crawled up the stairs, turned on my computer, and worked into the early morning hours creating the invitations. The next day, I made a few minor changes and started on the guest list. Though she'd affected so many lives, we were limited by funds and space. We kept the number of invitations to people who had closely impacted Izzy's life and mine.

The front of the invitations read:

You're Invited To Izabel's 8th Birthday Party

On the inside, Mom handwrote:

It's My Party and I'll Bark If I Want To!

The words were written in pink glitter, along with all the other significant details about the party. They were stuffed into an elegant envelope of silver foil and calligraphic lettering. You would have thought it was an invitation to a king's ball.

We decided to hold the party in the multi-purpose room at my church. This gave us all the room we needed to seat our guests comfortably. It also allowed ample room to celebrate both Izzy's big day and our anti-bullying work.

Friends and family helped to decorate early, so we'd be ready to welcome guests who were to arrive by noon. Laura painted a beautiful sign that matched the invitation and flowed around two walls of the room. It said, "It's My Party and I'll Bark If I Want To!"

To celebrate the book, I displayed many of the pictures, articles, and letters I had collected, along with information highlighting Izzy's and my speaking engagements. We played an anti-bullying song with photos of Izzy and me in the background and text messages at the bottom of each slide. One said, "Hands are for helping, not hitting." Another: "No one knows the weight of another's burden; be nice to everyone." In the picture, Izzy lay with her head on the floor, comfortably resting.

A TASTE OF IZZY'S PARTY: CHEX® MIX PUPPY CHOW RECIPE

We thought it would be fun to make "puppy chow" for all the tables. The recipe was on the back of the box of Chex Mix cereal. It really is good. You may want to think about trying it for your next party. It turned out to be a big hit at Izzy's.

Ingredients

9 cups Chex ®	1 teaspoon vanilla
1 cup butter	½ cup peanut butter
1 cup semisweet chocolate chips	½ cup powdered sugar

Directions

Put cereal in a large bowl. Put aside.

In another bowl, a microwavable one, place chocolate chips, peanut butter, and butter. Microwave chocolate, peanut butter and butter on high for 1 minute. Stir. Microwave for 30 seconds more or until the mixture is smooth. Stir in vanilla.

Pour mixture over Chex® cereal. Transfer mix into a large plastic bag with powdered sugar. Shake well to coat. Spread mixture evenly on wax paper to cool. Store in an airtight container.

Mom made several cakes in the shape of doggie bones, and I had Mom make Izzy a special bone-shaped cherry chip cake with cream cheese frosting. I laughed thinking about how happy Izzy would be to have something special on her birthday, especially since her normal diet consists only of Hill's Prescription k/d! Our local VG's Grocery was gracious enough to donate a large sheet cake for the rest of Izzy's guests.

Izzy was all decked out for her special day, with pink bows on each side of her long ears, her nails painted a frosty pink, and a beautiful variegated pink scarf tied around her neck. Izzy had been known as the pink girl since she was a pup when her breeder placed a pink ribbon around her neck to tell her apart from her brothers and sisters. I saw no reason to mess with a good thing. The color suited her, standing out against the backdrop of her shiny black and tan coat. Dom and Lindsay had been at all of Izzy's previous *smaller* birthday parties, so why shouldn't they come to Izzy's *Big Bash*? We dressed Dom in a blue shirt collar with a tie that hung to the floor—he almost tripped over it when he walked. Painted on the tie were colorful candles and party streamers. Lindsay Belle had pink bows in her hair and a black collar with white polka dots and four bright pink flowers attached to it. Everyone got a big kick out of their attire.

It was also a good time to see old friends and get caught up on the lives of others we dearly loved and appreciated. Izzy's "Grandma" Chris Hooker flew in from North Carolina the night before the party. It was great to see her. She, too, was so excited about the party, knowing in her heart that she had to be there. Izzy had created a bond between Chris and me, so the party was extra special to me, knowing Izzy's "Grandma" could attend.

Once everyone found a place to sit, I spoke briefly from my heart about what Izzy meant to me. I expressed my appreciation to all for taking the time to come to a dog's birthday party, which I knew must have seemed strange or unusual to many of them. I explained that to me she was more than a dog. She was my furry friend who gave me the unconditional love I needed to help me overcome my fears.

After I spoke, a treasured friend of ours we affectionately call "Grandpa Jesse" talked about his old dog and how dogs can be a tool to change a life.

Then, Mom took the opportunity to introduce Izzy's beautician and groomer, Kelly Davis. She has been a part of our lives for many years now, and, for more times than we want to admit, saved us when we had to rush Izzy in for a quick "make-over" for speaking engagements.

At the end of the party, Rick put Izzy on top of a round table next to her cake. Chris lit the candles while Rick held Izzy back. Dom and Lindsay sat in chairs at the table drooling for a piece of Izzy's cake. Once the candles were lit, everyone sang "Happy Birthday" to Izzy and laughed. It seemed so right! Everyone sang without hesitation. I blew the candles out for Izzy, and she gladly devoured her cake.

As the party wound down, I realized that it was everything I had hoped it would be and more. It only seemed right to honor my little girl in this way.

While at the party, someone told Mom that, in many cultures, the number eight stands for "New Beginnings." I was quick to remind her that, "Izzy's eight, I'm twenty-eight, and it's now 2008!"

Mom smiled as she said, "The joy is in the journey, Gabe. In doing what you are called to do, you'll see victories along the way. You know, this may be the year of the rainbow and all of our storms have passed."

She was right. Every day is a new day, filled with wonderful possibilities. I reached out to rub Izzy's soft ears as the party wound down and asked in that tone she seemed to dearly love, "Did you have fun, my Izzy girl?"

She gave me one of her understanding coondog looks, and I'm sure if she could speak, she would have said, "It's my party and I'll bark if I want to!"

"NO SCHOOL BULLYING!"

Gabe and Izzy Publishing

CHAPTER THIRTEEN

Year of the Rainbow

Shortly after Izzy's birthday party, Mom received an e-mail from our friend Mark Meckel in Nashville, Tennessee. During the Christmas holiday, Mark thought about Izzy and me and wondered how I'd feel about his writers working on a song, and possibly an entire CD of songs, that would help tell our story. Mark is the owner of MDM Records and Street Singer Music, a Grammy winning music publisher. He is also the manager for Dr. Monte Selby, a former elementary music teacher, middle school principal, and professor, who is now an international keynote speaker, workshop presenter, author, and recording artist. He uses humor, movement, interaction, and critically-acclaimed original music to inspire and motivate audiences all over the world. I'll forever cherish the day Monte and Mark stopped by our house in Fenton while on tour. It happened to be my birthday, so Monte sang a song to me. What a wonderful gift! Izzy and I are honored to call them our friends.

Mark, Mom, and I agreed that the first song should be universal in meaning, followed by a personal song about Izzy and me. A phone call was all it took to get his son Nathan Meckel and Burton Collins excited about the project. Nathan, a recording artist and producer, and Burton, a Grammy nominated writer, had collaborated on songs for years. They've written many cool songs for Monte, and since Nathan is also Monte's producer, it was only natural that they work on the project.

When Nathan and Burton sent me a rough recording of the song they called *"Hold On"* I was overjoyed. The positive lyrics rang in my ears.

> Time changes everything
> Nothing ever stays the same
> Lights are going to shine again
> Hold on, hold on.

This was the start of an entire CD of songs called Gabe & Izzy's Playlist complete with 10 songs of comfort and encouragement. I knew *"Hold On"* and the other songs would comfort not only me but many others who had been holding on for something positive in their lives.

It wasn't long after Mom's conversation with Mark that other opportunities followed. One day, the phone rang and the Caller I.D. showed a New York City area code. I let the call go to the answering machine. It was from *The Today Show* wanting to talk to Mom about Izzy and me.

I didn't get too excited yet because they only said they wanted to talk. Talking didn't mean they wanted to interview me. I occupied my mind with my normal business. When mom returned home from work and was relaxing on the sofa watching TV, I casually mentioned that *The Today Show* called.

She laughed and said, "Yeah, right, Gabe! I'm not falling for another one of your tricks."

Rick and I both tease Mom something fierce, and we're always playing jokes on her. I told her, "Go check the message yourself!"

Mom responded quickly, "I am not getting up. I'm not that gullible, Gabe. I've had a really busy day and need to rest right now."

Rick, who was also in the room, finally decided to hear for himself who had called. He got up off the sofa and pushed the play button on the recorder. In a reserved tone, he said, "She's not kidding, Rhonda Kay. They really did call and want you to call them ASAP."

Mom couldn't believe it. Neither could Rick. The initial phone call came on a Thursday; Mom called back on Friday, and by Tuesday of the next week a crew from *Today* stood in my living room. On that morning, the day after my twenty-eighth birthday, *The Today Show* producer Meredith Reis arrived at our home around 9 A.M. with correspondent Jenna Wolfe. Within the hour, the crew taped Jenna's interview with Mom and by noon, the crew had followed us to Lakeville High School in Otisville, Michigan to tape one of my school assemblies.

The Lakeville assembly went exceptionally well. The crew was amazed at how quiet and attentive the students were. Filming in a gymnasium can be challenging because noises echo and carry louder than in an auditorium. But in this gym, there wasn't a peep or squeak the whole time I was talking. The feedback from the question and answer period, student interviews, and observations after the assembly were remarkable. Even with all the excitement of *The Today Show* filming at their school, the message was getting through, and lives were being changed.

After the assembly, it was back to the house for more interviews. Donna, my co-writer, and her husband Steve had come to the house so the crew could film us working on this book. But first, the reporter would interview me, alone, in private.

The crew needed absolute silence, so Rick and Steve stayed in the living room with the French doors closed trying their best to keep the dogs quiet. This freed Mom and Donna up to eavesdrop on the foyer stairs to hear my broadcast interview. During our writing sessions we learned that Donna and Mom had much in common, including a love for laughter. The two giggled and whispered on the stairs during my interview like two schoolgirls. Several of my responses to Jenna's questions made them shed a few tears, but when our cat Sweetie crept down the stairs to check out the activities on the main floor, Mom and Donna were determined to keep the cat from disturbing the film session. The cat eventually escaped after some hilarious moments, which left Mom and Donna wondering what could possibly happen next.

The interview with Jenna was extensive and I will never forget how comfortable she made me feel. There is one particular question Jenna asked me during the interview that stands out in my mind. She wanted to know if I had a favorite quote.

The one I shared with her has been a favorite for some time:

> *"To the world you may be just be one person,*
> *But to one person you may be the world."*

I'll never forget the way Jenna lit up as she smiled. Although I've never had the chance to ask her, I believe she saw and understood the quote's meaning in my life.

The *Today* experience made me realize how much I had changed. It wasn't so long ago that I was afraid to leave the confines of home for fear of facing those who had bullied me in school. My love for Izzy changed all that. I used to be afraid of interviews and refused to have my photo taken in my wheelchair. Now I've had cameras pointed right at me and millions are seeing the photos. In truth, I am not ashamed of what I look like anymore.

The Today Show story aired on Good Friday and even while it was still airing, e-mails requesting booking information started coming in on my Web site. They continued throughout the day as the show crossed different cities and time zones.

Soon after, I was at my Aunt Jean's funeral in Indiana when Rick told Mom that *Cosmopolitan Magazine* had called and wanted her to call them back right away. After the service, she returned their call—and they wanted to interview me that day! Mom wanted to defer the interview to another day since we still had a funeral dinner to attend, but they mentioned having a deadline to meet. We agreed to do a phone interview later that afternoon. The article appeared in the inspirational section of the July 2008 issue.

Other magazines have done articles on Izzy and me as well, including *Guidepost*, *New Mobility* and one from out of the country, a Siberian health magazine called *VIVA*. The editor-in-chief, medical doctor and journalist Gradimir Joksimovic, wrote the story. Photos of Izzy and me were included with the article. I never received a copy of the magazine, but I did get the story as an e-mail attachment. Maybe one day I will have it translated into English!

The requests continue as a result of *The Today Show* airing. Schools and groups from all across the country have requested information on how they, too, can get me to come and speak to their group. Not only are schools requesting me, I've also spoken at a local Michigan Rotary Club and at the International Reading Association's Annual Convention in Phoenix, Arizona in February 2009. Twelve thousand people attended the convention in Phoenix, another reminder I've come a long way from speaking to groups of elementary school children in a school library. People call me a celebrity at times, but I just tell them, "I am not the celebrity, my dog is. I am just Gabe, a voice for the bullied." Without Izzy, I never would have become a voice that our nation's schools need.

Students across the nation are waking up and learning from my assemblies that bullying is a choice—witnesses are being empowered, schools are holding students accountable, and more and more schools have adopted a zero-tolerance anti-bullying policy. In my estimation, while we have by no means arrived, we have made great progress.

More surprises were around the corner. Sheila Smith called Mom and told her the Fenton Regional Chamber of Commerce wanted to honor me at a formal dinner on November 21, 2008. They wanted it to be a surprise, so Mom only told me that Sheila invited us to a Chamber of Commerce event. I had assumed only members of the Chamber of Commerce could receive an award, so when the ceremony began, it never occurred to me that I would be honored in this way. When they called my name, I'm sure my face turned three shades of cherry. As I made my way to the stage with Izzy, I began to shake. Not only did our Mayor, Sue Osborn, present the award to me, but Erin Maher, a friend from church, wrote a beautiful song for me and sang it for the first time directly to me that evening.

The song is called *The Dance*.

The award I received is called the Community Hero Award, and they played the clip from *The Today Show* at the event. What an honor.

I had another surprise to come. I finished this chapter and named it The Year of the Rainbow. Later that day, a huge rainbow appeared over the top of our home. You can imagine my astonishment. I knew then for sure that I'd chosen the perfect title. My neighbor Kevin McClure, who lives across the street, saw the rainbow and took a photo.

It was another blessing, another coincidence. He had no idea I was writing a book, let alone the fact that I completed this final chapter only a few hours earlier. I can't begin to describe the sense of confirmation I felt as I stared in amazement at the gift we received that day.

In my life, the winds of adversity tried to rob my family of our joy, but our faith remained strong, and those trials made us stronger. We held each other up through every storm and came through with a positive outlook. I can still hear Mom saying there would be a rainbow at the end of the storms, so we just kept holding on—refusing to let our ship capsize.

Friedreich's ataxia was not a welcome presence in my life, and, while it has weakened my body, it has also led me on a journey I would not trade for anything. Who would have ever guessed that someone like me, an unpopular outcast who had been bullied throughout her school years, would become known around the world for speaking out against the very thing that almost destroyed her?

Izzy came to me at a time when I desperately needed a friend—a friend who would love me unconditionally. Izzy's presence at assemblies is often the key that opens the hearts of students, enabling them to hear the message I'm presenting that is creating change.

I love seeing posters that read, "Izzy says, No School Bullying." Izzy really does have a voice. Her unconditional love is something she offers to everyone she meets, and I am told it speaks volumes.

I did not plan on becoming a national speaker, but I am one, and now I cannot imagine doing anything else. You see, there are hearts yet to be touched by the story I've been given. Although my dream of becoming a prima ballerina will never be realized, I am still dancing. My spirit dances within every time I appear before an assembly of people with my beloved Izzy by my side. My journey with Izzy has taught me that life isn't about waiting for the storms to pass, it's about learning how to dance during the rain. It's about waiting for the rainbows.

"NO SCHOOL BULLYING!"

Gabe and Izzy Publishing

CHAPTER FOURTEEN

Gabe's Anti-Bullying Messages for Kids, Parents and Educators

My story is about empathy, not sympathy. This was true when I was interviewed by Animal Planet and at each of my many speaking engagements. I don't seek sympathy for my disease or the bullying I endured. I seek empathy to show others how these things impacted me and how we can all treat each other differently.

If we are honest with ourselves, we'll admit that at some time in our lives we, too, have bullied or have witnessed someone being bullied and done nothing about it. The question is, are we willing to try and make this world a better place? If we make the effort, we can eliminate bullying and create a world where children can grow into healthy secure adults.

Educating people about bullying is a must. If one builds a house without a solid foundation, the house will not stand. The same is true with children. If they aren't taught that bullying is wrong, how will they ever become tolerant and respectful of other's differences? How will they ever create a culture of acceptance where bullying cannot thrive?

Bullying is a choice—a purposeful act. Everyone has to take responsibility for his or her own behavior. During my presentations at schools, I take a moment to address everyone who has a responsibility to stop bullying. I start with the children: those who bully, those who witness bullying, and the victim.

Do You Bully?

What you consider "messing around" another child might see as torment. You might not realize that your behavior is hurting others. Ask yourself the following questions to decide if your behavior is bullying behavior.

Have you ever . . .

. . . Pushed or shoved someone?

. . . Shut someone out? Refused to sit on the bus or at a lunch table with someone?

. . . Called someone a name?

. . . Criticized the way someone dressed or looked?

. . . Spread a rumor about someone that you didn't like?

. . . Asked someone else to tease someone or push someone?

. . . Treated someone in a way you wouldn't want to be treated yourself?

. . . Posted a negative comment on a blog or Web site about someone else?

. . . Sent a mean email, text or instant message to someone?

Did you answer yes to any of these questions? If so, you're just one of many children who may not realize that their behavior hurts others. Seek positive ways to interact with people and try to be kind when you see people who are different.

To the bully

Bullies are people who are cruel to people who are weaker than they are. Bullying is more than pushing or hitting. You might not think of yourself as a bully, but you are if you've ever called someone a name or made fun of someone who was different. You're a bully if you've ever pulled someone's hair or shot spit wads at that person. Many students don't realize they are bullies because they have never thought of themselves that way. They might see their actions as "messing around" and having fun but it is anything but fun for the one being targeted. Treating someone negatively or shutting them out of school events and activities can have a lifelong impact.

Many bully because it makes them feel powerful—they thrive on that power, that attention. Material things can be a driving force behind bullying. Bullies see something they want and take it from a weaker person. Perhaps they are merely acting out problems at home or copying the behavior of another classmate they admire. Some bullies crave attention, while others need to feel in control by winning at everything they do. The need to dominate others is a sure sign of a bully. They prey on insecure people. They would rather bully than chance being the one bullied. These students need to look deep inside themselves and ask the question, "Why am I acting this way?"

Bullies need to understand that this negative behavior can continue into adulthood. Many bullies lose their popularity as they get older, and the majority of students eventually dislike them. Some students will continue to struggle with anger issues and with groups, sometimes into adulthood.

These students will also need to grapple with the impact of their actions. I ask older students how they want to be remembered later in life when attending a high school reunion. I also share that when most students get older, they will look back over their school days and regret their actions if they made fun of other classmates. I stress, why live with regrets when you don't have to?

I encourage students to apologize to those to whom they have been cruel and they often do. I can't begin to tell you how many students have told me how freeing this is for both the bully and the victim. They feel good and less stressed believing bullying is over for them.

To those who witness bullying

Those who aren't bullied still have a responsibility to those who are. Don't keep silent because you want to protect yourself from being bullied or think it will win you points with a more popular crowd. A school is a community and students need to ask themselves if they want to live in a community where people get hurt. They need to dig deep inside and ask, "Do I want people treated like this in my school? Would I like my friends or my little sister to be shoved or snickered at or called names? Would it be ok if someone treated *me* like this?"

I encourage and lift up those who witness bullying to support the victim. The witness needs to feel empowered and feel strong enough to not laugh at the bully's actions and not contribute to the hurt a bully creates. When the witness doesn't chime in or help, bullies will feel weak and, more times than not, it will defuse their actions.

Sometimes the best way to defuse bullies is for witnesses to reach out to victims. Bullies target people who are alone and your presence can create safety in numbers. If you see kids who are always alone, go to them. Walk with them from the bus. Sit with them at lunch. Choose those people when you pick your teams in gym or other classes. Children who are teased dread coming to school and you will make that dread go away. You might even learn a little about those people and why they are different.

Witnesses also need to feel strong enough to reach out to a parent or educator if they see bullying occur. This isn't tattling on someone, this is making sure people in your school feel safe and secure.

All of us have good and bad qualities. We all have different interests and talents. It's important to develop our strengths, but in the process, we must be more accepting and tolerant of other's differences. Not everyone is going to be our cup of tea. We don't have to be best friends with people who are not, but neither should we accept a culture that makes fun of people.

ARE YOUR CHILDREN BEING BULLIED?

Not all parents realize that their children are being bullied. Some children feel embarrassed telling anyone about the teasing or the tormenting they've endured. Additionally, parental love can blind people to the realities that their child is disliked or treated poorly. Read the following for signs you might recognize in your child.

Do your children . . .

. . . Request to stay home when they aren't sick.
. . . Request to be excused from certain classes.
. . . Act withdrawn or quiet.
. . . Avoid areas where other children might be: bus stops, school events, extracurricular activities.

If you see any of these signs in your children, act quickly. Talk to your children alone and make them feel as comfortable as possible. Mention that you've noticed some changes and you'd like to talk about them. Whether your children can talk then or another day, make sure they feel safe opening up to you.

To the victim

Because everyone is responsible for his or her actions, the victim has an important responsibility as well: To forgive.

Earlier in the book, I told you about a boy who punched me in the leg, among other things. He stopped bullying me when he understood the impact he had on me. My willingness to forgive him helped me to go on. If only I could have understood then what I do now.

I have forgiven those who have bullied me, and I tell students they should do the same, even if the offending party never apologizes. Forgiving others will help you as a person to release the anger and bitterness that could otherwise destroy you. Forgiveness is healing. When you forgive, it helps the one forgiving more than the one who is being forgiven.

Habitually cruel individuals need help, and we need to have empathy for them. Many times bullies were once bullied themselves. One would think the way it made them feel would be enough to bring change, but that is not

---

ARE YOU BEING BULLIED?
WHAT TO DO (AND WHAT NOT TO DO)

Getting bullied? You might feel helpless, but you don't need to. There's hope and through communication and positive outreach you can stop the bullying and improve your life.

Do reach out to someone. Find teachers, educators or parents you trust and tell them what has been happening to you.

Don't think the bullying will just go away.

Do join extracurricular activities or clubs with kids you enjoy. You shouldn't let the bully take the fun from your life.

Don't avoid the world. Don't skip school or avoid classes. Don't let those bullies take your education, too!

Do stand up for yourself, if you feel safe. Bullies thrive on fear. Ask them to stop their behavior and be confident.

Don't bully back. Don't push or shove or call names. Be above that bully's behavior.

Do be positive. It's not your fault you are being bullied and eventually the bullying will end.

Don't hurt yourself. You might become sad or depressed and want to hurt yourself because you think there's no other answer, but there is. Go to an adult and find help.

---

always the case. Perhaps they are insecure because they have been bullied in their homes, or maybe they are just looking for attention. We may never know why they do what they do. They might not want to change, but what if they do and they just don't know how? One never knows the kind of impact we can have on bullies when we're willing to tell them how their actions make us feel and give them the opportunity to change.

I think it's also important to speak directly to parents and educators due to their role in guiding students toward proper behavior.

To the parents

Parents need to set standards of behavior. These standards should be clearly defined for children in and out of school. Parents can encourage their children to help others. If they witness bullying, they should act immediately and appropriately and inform an adult. They should teach their children not to join in but to have respect for other's differences. Parents should share stories from their own childhood about good and bad situations. Those stories will come alive in their hearts and minds and are examples from which their children can learn.

If a child accuses their child of bullying, parents need to listen with open ears. Don't dismiss roughhousing or teasing as "kids will be kids." Even good children make bad choices. A parent or educator who comes to you with a bullying concern is not telling you that your child is bad or judging your parenting abilities. In fact, that parent or educator is giving you a chance to show how great a parent you are by listening to the situation and correcting a negative behavior. Your children need to see that you take these issues seriously so that they have incentive to change their behavior.

If you suspect your children are bullied, encourage them to reach out to you so you can then reach out to others, such as educators and the other child's parents. Your child needs to feel comfortable coming to you with problems and seeing that communication can bring about a positive change.

Parents need to examine their own behavior as well. Think about how you react to people from different social, economic or racial backgrounds.

Think about jokes you might tell to your adult friends that you don't think your child can hear. When you ridicule people or groups for being different, you teach your child that ridiculing people is acceptable behavior.

If you see television shows or movies that ridicule characters for being different, that is an opportunity to teach your children acceptance. It does

---

For Parents and Educators: Helping the Victim

Adults who see children struggling with bullying are often at a loss to know how to help. Take a look at these tips from the U.S. Department of Health and Human Services site:

Stop Bullying Now!
(www.stopbullyingnow.hrsa.gov) for guidance.

- Be Discrete. Be careful to give too much public support since kids are wary of what other kids see and know.

- Learn what's going on. Find out how long the bullying has been going on, who is doing the bullying and what the victim thinks about it.

- Build the student up. Students should know that they have been courageous to come forward and that this will help other students as well as themselves.

- Make sure the student feels safe. If the student wants confidentiality, grant it. If this student just wants an ear, be that ear. If you confront the bully or talk with other educators or parents, make sure that the victim's identity is protected.

- Talk with other adults. Other educators and parents can provide help and advice. They can also observe the situation and help prevent further incidents.

- Help the student find a support system. Finding friends and confiding in parents ensures that victims don't feel alone.

not matter if we are short, tall, thin, overweight, have a scar, have different color skin, different texture and color of hair, are part of a different religion, or are physically or mentally disabled. We need to learn to be more accepting of other people's differences and understand that this is a wonderful thing. Think about it: if we were all the same, wouldn't it be a really boring world?

To educators

There are many reasons educators must take action against bullying. Look at the recent incidents of school violence. Often, it is the victims of bullying who are frustrated who turn to revenge. In addition, children who are repeatedly bullied are at greater risk of committing suicide. They feel hopeless and see death as their only means of escape.

Bullying is one of the most underrated and enduring problems in schools today. Schools are a prime location for bullies to thrive. Every child has a right to be educated and feel safe at school. Those working in the educational system must enforce a safe environment. It's their duty.

I urge schools to foster an anti-bullying culture. Often, this starts with education for students and educators. Many curriculums are available for schools willing to give their teachers and counselors the tools they need. Presentations, like mine, can be instrumental to students needing to change their behavior. But educators need to be vigilant after the assemblies end to ensure that every child is treated with respect.

The demand for me to speak across the country has continued to soar. Thousands of students and teachers have expressed how much they enjoy my presentation. I'm lucky that I have managed the courage and determination to speak out and share my story. Many students aren't so lucky and suffer in silence. By fighting bullying, one school at a time, we can ensure that no students need to suffer any longer.

"NO SCHOOL BULLYING!"
Gabe and Izzy Publishing

Resources

C hange starts with education. Take a look at these sites to learn more about me, bullying awareness and Friedreich's Ataxia.

1. The Official Site of Gabrielle Nicole Ford
Web site: Gabeandizzy.com

Learn more about her anti-bullying campaign and find out where she's speaking next. Leave a message on her online guestbook, book her for your own school or group, or buy the inspirational CD mentioned in the book for a friend in need.

2. Bullying
Center for the Study and Prevention of Violence
Web site: www.colorado.edu/cspv/resources/links.html#Bullying

A clearinghouse of information for educators, parents and students on school violence and bullying.

15+ Make time to Listen, Make Time to Talk
Web site: www.mentalhealth.samhsa.gov/15plus

Provided by the Department of Substance Abuse and Mental Health Services Administration, this campaign is based on the idea that parents who talk with their children for 15 minutes or more are better able to help those children build positive relationships. The site offers free publications on dealing with and preventing bullying for parents, educators, caregivers, teens and children.

Stop Bullying Now!
Web site: www.Stopbullyingnow.hrsa.gov
This Web site, created by the U.S. Department of Health and Human Services' Health Resources and Services Administration offers a kids' page with tips on dealing with bullies, games and webisodes. It also offers a page for adults with tip sheets, state law information and discussion guides.

3. *Friedreich's ataxia (FA)*
Friedreich's Ataxia Research Alliance (FARA)
Web site: www.CureFA.org
This national non-profit seeks to cure Friedreich's ataxia through research. Look to this site for results from new studies and trials.

National Ataxia Foundation (NAF)
Web site: **www.ataxia.org**
A non-profit, the NAF improves the lives of those impacted by FA through support, education and research. This site provides links to support groups, events, research and chat rooms.

Muscular Dystrophy Association (MDA)
Web site: **www.mda.org**
This non-profit health agency aims to cure muscular dystrophy, ALS and related diseases through funding and worldwide research. Look to this site for fact sheets on various neuro-muscular diseases, to find clinics or support groups near you, and to connect with other families impacted by neuro-muscular diseases.

LIVES TOUCHED

Posted Comments to www.gabeandizzy.com

The testimonials I have received are a steady reminder of the impact of my efforts. Hearing about the struggles and obstacles I had to overcome has touched students, parents and educators deeply. Thesc letters have touched me deeply as well and are the inspiration for me to continue with motivational speaking. Here is a sample of letters from my online guestbook.

Posted by Sean on September 22, 2003 01:30 AM

Hey Gabe, You have made a difference in my life . . . You and your mom, and ol' droopy ears, and all the other characters that make your life so amazing and who make me so fortunate to have met you. You're such a positive and strong person, and damn, you have a good taste in music too, girl! I'm excited that Samji will also get to meet a special dog. Maybe Iz can teach her not to chew on furniture!

I've gotta tell you Gabe, you're leaving beautiful footprints that no one who has the pleasure of meeting you will ever forget.

Posted by Hayley on December 14, 2004 01:37 PM

Today, you and Izzy visited my school, Hartland Ore Creek. I thought that the presentation would be just another "No bullying" or "Stay drug-free" assembly but this was different. I liked hearing from someone who actually knew what she was talking about. I talked to you after the presentation and asked you what it was like when you found out that you were no longer able to dance. I know, and told you, that if I found out I couldn't dance anymore, I would be completely heartbroken. I would like you and your mom to know that from now on, I will be dancing for you. God bless you and Izzy.

Posted by Amanda on May 30, 2005 09:36 AM

Gabe, you had a very touching story, and was felt by many people in my school. You were recently at my school, in Lansing, New York. I know one bully (well, one former bully). Just hearing you speak that day made her realize that what she was doing was wrong, and she apologized to all those people to whom she'd been so mean, myself included. You left a long lasting impression on a lot of those bullies here in Lansing, and I wanted to thank you for it. It must have taken a lot of guts to go up there and speak to us, but you did a great job.

Posted by Michele on October 24, 2005 04:40 PM

I would like to thank you for coming to Springton Lake Middle School on October 24th. I'm in the 7th grade and even though we have a bully prevention program, that didn't seem to stop the many bullies at my school. After you spoke, I went to the hall to see everybody apologizing and being nice to each other. Your talk about your personal experience made a huge impact on everyone at my school. Thank you so much for helping us become a better place. Say "Hi" to Izzy for me.

Posted by Nicole on October 24, 2005 05:57 PM

I saw the assembly today at Springton Lake Middle School. I'm in the 7th grade. I just wanted to say that Izzy is so cute! Your story touched me so much that I cried. I actually did say sorry to the people who I bullied because what you said was true, that bullying will scar people for life or at least for a long time. I hope that you write back! Thanks so much for coming to our school.

Posted by Nancy on October 28, 2005 05:51 PM

Thank you so much for coming to Marticville Middle School on very short notice today! Your presentation was exactly what our kids needed to hear, and I wasn't the only one with teary eyes after watching your video. Now we have an excellent reference point when we are talking to our students about bullying: "Remember when Gabe and Izzy came to talk to us . . .?" You will certainly make a difference in the lives of many of our students. Bless you for caring enough to make this heroic effort to share your story!

Posted by Anna on November 15, 2005 10:32 AM

Gabe, I really think that you are right, that no one deserves to be bullied. I don't know why anyone would bully you, I mean, you're pretty, and it surprises me that people were mean to you. I know how you feel about being bullied. People bully me because they think that I'm ugly. I'm really tall so my pants are always too short on me. People also are mean to me because of that. I know I'm pretty, but people still call me ugly. I really liked your slideshow too. I think that the song was so nice. It really touched me.

Posted by Kaye on January 27, 2006 04:38 PM

I just wanted to tell you thank you for coming to our school. I thought you really changed everything around and made my day because when my class left the gym and got back to the classroom they all said they were sorry for all the pain they have caused me by calling me names.

———————————

Posted by Jillian and Alenah on Feb. 25, 2006 06:20 PM

We were really touched by your story and we wanted to know how you were doing! Our school really recovered from all that bullying! Before you came to our school all we heard were swear words and there were a lot of fights and people pushing and shoving. So we just wanted to say thank you for coming and sharing your story about your life that really touched everyone!

———————————

Posted by Tracey on January 22, 2007 06:25 PM

Thank you for coming to Carleton Middle School, in Sterling Heights, Michigan and spreading the message about no bullying. Your story is extremely powerful and made everyone around me have tears in their eyes. Thank you for showing the students that they have a voice and that they need to use it. You are an inspiration to many and you just added 600 students to your fan club.

———————————

Posted by Linda on August 18, 2007 10:02 AM

I am a teacher at South Vermillion Middle School. Today I met Gabrielle and Izzy . . . and my life is changed. In my 30 years of teaching, I have never been as inspired as I was today by anyone. I will cherish the picture my school took of Gabe, Izzy and me. It will remind me of what real strength and determination is all about. Gabe is a truly remarkable young woman, and I know, as a mother, how very proud and blessed you are to have her for your daughter.

———————————

Posted by Kevin on May 17, 2007 06:16 PM

I really loved your talk with the Barre Town School. I really enjoyed it and I hope every one else did. I wish that I could help make your dreams come true, but I know that it can't be changed or get better. I also learned a lot from your talk. I like fooling around with kids like the way you got bullied. When you talked about it I felt bad and I said sorry to a lot of those kids to whom I'd been mean, and I never knew that it was bullying. Now that you have taught me all that good stuff I am going to stop doing what I did to bully kids.

Posted by Keely on September 4, 2007 06:55 PM

I am in the 4th grade on Mackinac Island and I think it was really great you could make it up to the Island and speak to us. I won't be a bully and I will stick up for other kids who are getting picked on and be their friend. I hope Izzy is with you for a long time and I hope you both had a wonderful time on the Island.

Posted by Alyssa on September 20, 2007 08:19 PM

I hope you have fun going all around the world to schools to talk about bullying! P.S. I made a new friend because she was being bullied and playing by herself. She is so nice.

Posted by Tyler on October 28, 2007 04:28 PM

The day you guys came and had the assembly, I told my parents that people were bullying me. They did something about it. You gave me courage.

Posted by Emily on November 8, 2007 06:57 PM

I was at the school that you just visited (Franklin Monroe Elementary, in Ohio). I really liked how you talked about how your schoolhood was. I really liked the video. Although it was very sad, I liked it. I have bullied some people in school, and I've gone along with my friends whenever they did it.

But I want you to know that you changed my life by telling about how you were bullied and I'm going to say sorry to the people I bullied. I will stand up for other people too. Pet Izzy for me!

Posted by Samantha on November 30, 2007 05:14 PM

You came to my school on Friday, November 30. You are the best and you made the biggest bully in the sixth grade cry. She was so amazed how bullying can impact people's lives so much.

Posted by Tamara on December 3, 2007 05:34 PM

I live in Madison, Indiana. I really need to tell you how amazing you are and what you have done for me. My son goes to the school you and your mother spoke at on Friday. My son Ryan is 14 and somehow, someway, you really touched him. He is a good kid deep down. I have always tried to instill in him to always treat others the way you want to be treated. Friday he came home and told me all about you and I just wanted to tell you, please keep doing what you're doing, because it really does help these kids learn. Ryan gets in trouble a lot for being loud and very outspoken and I remember a teacher telling me last year that there was a good boy in there somewhere and she was going to find him. Well, I know you found him. You are a beautiful woman with a heart of steel and I thank you for that.

Posted by Jayla on April 17, 2008 1:23 PM

I just wanted to let you know, that after you came to our school (Scarlett Middle School) there were so many "sorrys" going through the hallway. You have inspired us all to do the right thing and stop bullying. The school is much better now ever since you came.

Posted by Mindze on April 17, 2008 5:43 PM

You came to our school today, Scarlett Middle School. And I just wanted to tell you that your message really touched my heart. I have a habit of playfully saying things that I know would not be things I would want people to say to me. But then you talked to us today about how sometimes we don't know it but we are hurting people. I'm going to try my hardest to stop, because I never realized that it might hurt someone. Thank you for helping me to see this.

Posted by Allayah on April 17, 2008 6:12 PM

Thanks for inspiring people to say sorry to me and everybody who made fun of somebody. I went through what you went through. Everybody calls me duck face and only a few people said sorry. But I want to thank you for everything. . . . Your words touched me and I hope you and Izzy make it and get through the troubles you have. Even though you and Izzy have a disease you both are beautiful inside and out.

Posted by Bailey on April 17, 2008 6:56 PM

I know how you feel with Izzy when she was diagnosed with the liver disease. I had a dog and she was a golden retriever. She had lockjaw and she got a muscle disease in her neck. We took her to the vet all the time. She was a very good dog. I loved her to death. But unfortunately when I came home one day, I found out that she had died. And with the bullying, I am bullied all the time and no one wants to stand up for me because I act different than the other kids. I have a few friends, but they don't like hanging out with me a lot. They are good friends, but they are trying to fit in with the cool kids and I am never welcomed into that group. They pick on me when the cool kids are around. I lock myself in my house and the day goes by fast and another day goes by before my eyes. You really have inspired me and I want to say thank you so much, Gabe and Izzy.

Posted by Samantha on April 17, 2008 7:26 PM

Wow, your videos made me tear up. I definitely learned a lot and thought about if I have ever bullied anyone before. Then at lunch, I saw one of the popular jock kids talking to you and I could tell you really sent him a message. It was a big surprise. I loved the assembly.

———————————————

Posted by Heather on May 1, 2008 4:39 PM

You came to my school and everyone loved your speech. You have made a big difference in my life. I get very frustrated with people very easily and I take stuff out on other people because of problems at home. I know I should not but it just happens. A lot of kids make fun of other people and it's not right. I am starting to realize that it does hurt other people's feelings and I stopped after your speech. So thank you so much for taking the time to do the right things for others.

I'm so sorry that this happened to you. But think about it—you're still the same nice and generous person you were 16 years ago and I just wanted to tell you thank you and you're such a great person.

———————————————

Posted by Emily on May 1, 2008 6:32 PM

I used to bully this one girl and I guess I never really knew how she felt about it. After today, I came up to her and told her I was sorry about how I treated her. Thank you for coming to Richmond High School today!

———————————————

Posted by Jackson Ryan on May 1, 2008 8:45 PM

You told my school about bullying and I just wanted to say that you changed my life completely. . . . I am a 12-year-old boy and have three kids who always push me around. After your speech all three came up to me and said they were sorry they pushed me around and called me names. I thought to myself, "Should I really believe this is really happening?" So you have inspired me to live by a motto and I hope you like it: "Live each day like it is your last." I have become a nicer and more driven individual. I loved your speech and if I could I would like to hear it over and over again. I wish I could help you talk about bullying so that more people know that bullying is bad. I also wanted to say you don't look your age. You don't look a day over 18.

Also, I wanted to say thank you for the hug and I think you are really nice and pretty. Tell Izzy that I said, "Hi." I will never forget what you said and you will always be a big part of my life. I hope you have a good life because I do and I hope Izzy is around for many years.

Posted by Olivia on May 31, 2008 10:43 AM

On Friday, May 30, you visited my school. I loved the assembly. My older brother has autism (have you heard of it?) and he is in high school. He gets bullied all the time. Sometimes when my brother and me are in public, people look at him and laugh. I yell at them and tell other adults, including teachers. Am I doing this action correctly?

Posted by Melanie on June 12, 2008 3:41 PM

Gabe, thank you so much for coming to our school and bringing Izzy. I think that it is safe to say that you truly inspired many people at our school. Your story was touching to all of us, and I even cried the day they showed us the Animal Planet video. I know your speech was effective because all day long, all I heard was, "I'm sorry for hurting you that day," and "It's alright. Thanks for apologizing." So, that means that this speech was very helpful. So, thanks again.

Posted by Derrick on June 23, 2008 10:32 AM

You are right about everything. Bullying is wrong. I get bullied some-times and I don't like it. I told them to go to your Web site and they said that they were sorry. I thank you for making the school visits. If you did not do the school visits I would still be getting bullied.

Posted by Taina on June 13, 2008 5:00 PM

Gabe, I think you have made a difference to my school. Thanks a bunch!! After we left the assembly a lot of the class bullies apologized to my friends and me. We appreciate you for making a difference in the world.

Posted by Chelsea on June 12, 2008 6:51 PM

Thank you for coming to our school and sharing your story with us. I honestly appreciated it and it really meant something to me. In your speech you said to apologize to someone you picked on today because there might not be a tomorrow. Well, guess what? I did. I went up to the girl and had a huge conversation on how sorry I am. She forgave me and now we say "hi" to each other in the hallway. You honestly touched my heart and made me rethink my actions. Tonight, when I say my prayers I am going to include you and Izzy and ask God to help everyone out in the world find a way to live and love life just like you. Thank you for everything.

P.S. Everyone in school today was really nice to everyone especially in lunch today . . . I think it is because you touched all of us. Please feel free to e-mail me if you want when you have time because I don't want to forget about you and I have some questions I want to ask you. Thank you.

Acknowledgements

This book would not have been possible without Bob Urban and Chris Hooker, Izzy's breeders. Thank you for your part in fulfilling my dream of owning a female coonhound with extra long ears. Because of you I met my special furry girl, Izzy. I am also grateful to Dr. Sandy Smith and her staff at Animal Health Clinic. You cared for Izzy as if she were your own. You're the best.

I send a huge thank you to the citizens of Fenton for their love and support. Saving my dog's life was my heart's cry and you responded valiantly. You understood Izzy's impact on my life and donated funds to help pay her extensive medical bills. I will never forget your kindness. A very special thanks goes out to the Fenton Chamber of Commerce. I will cherish my award and proclamation forever!

To the wonderful doctors who helped Rick and my mother through their battles with cancer: Dr. C. Hawker, Dr. K. Geran, Dr. J. Cabell and his wife Debbie, and their staffs. Thank you also to the Family Doctor's Clinic, Dr. E. J. Daros and his wife Jackie Daros, Dr. Anthony Daros, and Dr. Darla Murphy. You've always been there for my family. You're all very special to me.

Thanks to Barb LaPointe, Pat Schleh, Sandy Matthee, Nancy Rowe, Margie Bergren, Jane Rauch, Janelle Dowdle, Jackie Acs, Shelly Coad, Kelly Burgess, Roger Davis, Laura Ouellette, Debbie Wheeler, Shelia Smith, Becky Bugala, Davette Shelton, Marcie Carpenter, Barb Warden, John Spencer, Kace Wakem, Cathy and Dave Ehred, Steve and Emily Curiak, and the Freedom Center and Cornerstone Church friends who brought meals to my family to save my mom from cooking during busy times.

My dear friend Amanda, you and your family have given me a treasure chest of wonderful memories. I was privileged to be your maid of honor and then to have your daughter Allison born on my birthday—how special!

Sean Nasri, you are a true friend, someone I can talk to and trust. I'm so glad you tracked me down after seeing me Animal Planet's *A Pet Story*.

Thanks to those Lake Fenton students who had the courage to stand up for me while I was being bullied. Your kindness did not go unnoticed and will never be forgotten.

To Tracy Stimac, thanks for going out of your way while I was at Lake Fenton to teach students about people who are different. Beth Thomas and Mr. Miller, you were always so nice to me during my school days. Thanks! I will never forget you.

The students, educators, and friends who have taken the time to write me make my journey worthwhile. The letters and comments have encouraged me and given me strength to continue my work in schools and other places. Knowing my life's journey with Izzy has made a positive difference in the lives of so many has helped me to keep moving toward my goal—teaching the youth and others to build a more empathetic society.

I would like to thank Dominik Hasek, a former Detroit Red Wing (NHL goaltender), and Dale Johnson CEO of Dominator Clothing (www.dominatorclothing.com) and wife Erica for the Dominator clothing you provided for me. Thank you for believing in my mission.

To my canine friends Lindsey Belle and Dominik, and her feline friends Sweetie and Bob: You have always being there to cuddle with me during lonely times. All of you are such a comfort and a huge part of my life.

Donna Rhine, thanks for the close friendship we've developed while writing this book. We sure did laugh a lot. I will cherish those days forever. The meals you made to keep us going were so yummy!

To Linda Lacina: Thanks for your editorial expertise.

I send heartfelt thanks to my best friend Izzy, who I believe has taken on an illness similar to my own as a part of her caregiving nature. I stumble and so does Izzy. Izzy's unconditional love has propelled me into what I am doing today. She, my hero, has given me wings to fly higher than I could have ever imagined. My heart's desire is that Izzy will live forever—now she will in the hearts and lives of those touched by our story.

I send special thanks to my family who has been supportive in so many ways. The sacrifices you've made have not gone unnoticed. Caitlin, Madeline, Aunt Linda, Uncle Bob, Robbie, Tracy, Uncle Steve, and Emily: thanks so much for loving me and always being there.

To Papa who still lives with us and Mimma who went home to be with the Lord, thanks for your unconditional love. Papa, you're always doing thoughtful things like making sure my ramp is shoveled so I can get to the car for my events, and waiting in the driveway to help me into the car. Your loving care is a gift. Thanks so much, Papa.

An extra special thanks to Rick who wasn't afraid to marry my mom knowing I had a disability. He's a very special man who makes me laugh and has gone out of his way to love me for who I am, never making me feel like a burden. He sees me—not my disability.

Mom, how can I ever thank you enough for your loving support throughout my life. You never gave up on me, calling yourself a blessed woman because God entrusted me to you. The mission Izzy and I are on could not move forward without you. I know how much time you have given up to help me in this endeavor. I will never forget the countless hours you spent driving Izzy and me across the United States to share my story with others. The traffic delays, rain, ice, and snowstorms try to keep us from reaching our destinations on time, but nothing deters you. Thanks for believing in me and helping to make a difference in the lives of others. Students are opening their hearts, looking beyond my disability, and hearing my message because of you. I love you Mom. Thank you!

APPENDIX

Handwritten Letters

Dear Gabe and Izzy,
Thank you for visiting us and talking to us about school bullying. I promise never to bully any school kid. I promise I will never judge a person.

Love,
Mary

P.S. hope you like the pictures.

Gabe & Izzy are the best!!

October 24, 2005

Dear Gabe and Izzy,

You guys taught me so much. I am bullied, but not abt so I don't tell anyone, but you taught me that I should. You also taught me that maybe I should watch what I say. Everyone says that I'm nice, but maybe I'm not as nice as I think, and should watch what I do and say. I enjoyed listening to you talk. I thought that it was cool of you to talk to us, even if you have trouble talking. You made me feel a bit braver about being bullied and telling someone. I also enjoyed meeting you and Izzy and I hope to see you both again someday!!

Thanks for talking to us! Thanks for driving as far as you did just to help us. I will always remember you both.

Sincerely,
Shannon

October 24, 2005

Dear Gabe and Izzy,

I'm very glad you come to our school. Your assembly really made me think about bullying. It taught me that bullying can scare someone for life, and that no matter what the case you should never do it. It also taught me to report bullying the next time I see it, and I see it often. I'm going to report bullying the next time I see it because I don't want someone to feel alone like Gabe did.

Thank you for coming to our school to speak to us. I will carry some of the things you and your mother said with me for life!

I only have one question for you. Do you miss the sports you used to do often?

Sincerely,
Kayla

Dear Gabe and Izzy,
Thankyou Gabe and Izzy for coming to our school to tell us your message. Your message was great. You should go to other schools to encourage them to use your message. I will not bully any people because of your message.

Sinceraly,
Jake

Dear Grabrielle and IZZY, Thank you for kitting us pet the dog. We learned a lot about wtat is right and wtat is not.

Gabe We know How you feel! YOU too Izzy!

A poem for Gabe! you:

Never give up no matter how hard you try. Keep going or life will Pass you by. Never give up EVER! And never say NEVERT!! What ever you do!

NO BULLI

Dear Gabe and Izzy,
I really enjoyed your visit. Your story touched my hart. People can be so careless. I hope one day they can find a cure for your condition.

best of luck
Olivia

G B & IZZY

Age: 10

IZZY

Dear Gabe and Izzy,
Thank you for coming to
Rio School. I learned that when a
person gets bullied, the hurt can
last for many years. I also learned
if someone is being bullied I should
tell my parents or teachers. My
sister calls me names all the time.

Name Jessica C

Dear Gale and Izzy,

Thank you very much for coming to Rio Elementry school. I feel very sorry for you. It was proubly alot to go through. I learned that bullying can last a long long time after it stops. I also learned that if you're getting bullied you should tell someone and calling names can hurt alot. Even though a person doesn't show that they're hurt there proubly very hurt. I'm very happy you found Izzy.

Sincerely, Jessica C

Thank you for coming to our school. Your speech really touched my heart. Please do come again.

Dear Gabe,

I seen your episode on Animal Planet 2·23·04 prior to Ms. Hillmans tape. My mom was telling me why you were on the show and how she enjoyed watching it. She watched the episode 3 times. Seeing that episode, and talking to the class really changed on how I think and act around people. I never bullied anyone for anything, but I do know how it feels to be in your situation back then.

You are so strong for staying in school and finishing even with the bullying, that also had an effect on me personaly. When I used to get bullied, I would try to stay strong, but my anger opened me up and I stood up for myself and got suspended. So in your case it really makes you strong for not getting out of hand when bullied.

I love your dog! I would take him in a second. Thank You so much for staying strong and for coming to our school and sharing your lives with us. It really means alot. Good luck and may your wishes come true.

Dear Gabe and
Izzy Thank you
for letting us pet
Izzy. and coming to
our. school and
teaching us about
bullying. We learned
a lot from you.

love: J

February 23, 2004

Dear Gabe,

Thank you for comming to our school and telling us your story. It really helped open my eye's to see the effect of bullying. Before you came to are school I never pay ditton to Bullying, I kinda over looked it. Now when I see sumeone getting Bullied I Jump in and stop it. It is a really good thing you du for kids by going to all the different schools. Im sure that it helps stop alot of bullying.

Dear Gabe,   Feb. 23. 04

      Thankyou for coming
to our class and seeing us.
It made me appreciate the little
things more, I truly believe you
are a strong person and you are
here for a reason. You made me
take a step back + realize that
maybe the way I treat people
sometimes is a little unfair. I
wish you the best in the
future, and Izzy to. Goodluck
with the children's books also.
              Thank you,

Dear Gabe,

   I was honored being able to meet you in
person and hear about your journey. Let me
say that I think you're an amazing person
to be able to carry on the way you are.
Not most people in situations similar to yours
would have accepted it and try to make the
best of everything. If anyone were in search
to better themselves and attitude they should
learn from you.
   Gabe, you have inspired me more than
anyone I know and I could of. I have been
trying to be a better person and trying
to be alot more positive. It's been working but
ever since I've heard your story it has made
my 'changing' alot more easier. Thank you
for being the wonderful, strong, and brave
person that you are.
   I think I can relate to you situation
somewhat for I had battled cancer for
four years I have been cancer free for three
years now but still it's distressing to know
that I have a big chance for being taken
over by cancer again. You have made
me strong and to not worry. I was
touched by your story, will, determination,
and bravery more than you can know.
My prayers are with you as well as my
good thoughts. Stay strong, Gabe, for you
are certainly an angel on earth.

I want it to say thank you four coming to are Shool. Anyways i Also wan it to say that you Change my acts and you open my eyes more And the fack you open My heart.

You are really prety Gurl and no mater what People say about you Is not tru because you are the Biger person In life and I wish you So much luck and tak care.

I am so happy you came to are skool, I Love the way you open my oyez And my heart.

by:
GAbE
-3-
1
Izzy

tAke kare

Love ya

Dear Gabe,   2-23-04
        First I would like to say thank you For coming to our Class and speaking. It was really nice to have you. Izzy is a good dog. She so cute. I love her floppy ears.
        Your story is very insperational. I mean I dont know if I have ever really picked on Anyone, I'm sure I have, everyone has. but I know I've laghed at people and I knew but I understand more now that even though it might seem like just fun. You can really hurt someones feelings.
        Thank you again for coming to our class

                              Always.

Dear gabe,

I hope you and izzy don't give up hope.

Dear Gabe,

I know how you feel. And that is very unselfish how you don't like to feel bad for yourself! I'm excited to get to meet you!

Dear Gabe   February 23 2009

I would like to Thank for coming into our class and talking about yourself and your dog. I honestly believe that you are an amazing and brave person. The day you came in and talked to us you really inspired me deeply. I know you don't like it when people feel bad for which when I first watched the movie I did, but then I realized that we don't have to feel bad, we should feel more proud of what you have done and forget about the disease as much as we can because in some ways its not important. Having fun and being with the people you love or animals that you love. From high school being teased and stuff like that I think that you are very strong for going out in public and realizing that the people who teased you are not at all worth caring what they think. The soft hearted person you are trough it is very hard to look over it, I know I could not have done it. Gabe you have just inspired me so much you have no idea and how your dog Izzy came to you it was like a miracle, so amazing. I hope you had fun when you came + your mom + little sister and Izzy, Thank you for coming and talking to us. I wish you

---

Hey,

No matter what anyone says, you are the cool kid, both of you. And you two are, in my opinion, angels from heaven sent to help millions of kids with their Bulling problem. And I truely mean that from the bottom of my heart!

You and Izzy truely have something special.

Love is truely hard to find and you guys are the lucky ones that found it!

You guys inspire me to do good and be the best that I can possible be.

Hey Gabe + Izzy,

I wanted to thank you guys for coming. In the past I was a bully and after what you said I feel terrible. Also, Izzy you are an incredible dog and if it weren't for you I wouldn't of change my way of thinking on bullies.

As soon as I get out of here you guys will be hereing from me because I want to learn how to be more like Izzy and Gabe

Dear Gabe,

Hi, I really appreciated you coming in to talk to our 3rd hour English Class. Its great that even though you had such a hard time in school with people, you can come out in the open talk about it, and how it effects your life. I think that takes alot of guts. I also think that its people like you that inspire other people to talk about it. To realize just because that you may look different, that doesnt mean anything! I personally do not have a desese or anything that could effect my body image, but I know that, if I did, I wouldn't be ashamed.

Your dog Izzy is so lovely. I understand how a dog can make you feel better. By always being there for you and keeping you company. I have a Jack Russel at home named Darci and she is really important to me. I dont know what I would do without her. Again thank you for coming to visit us and I hope you come again

Dear Gabe,

I'm glad that you came to our school and shared your story with us. I think you are so brave to go out and tell everyone how you feel, and how you found Izzy. I've been bullied too, pretty much all of my life. I used to hate to come to school because of bullys now I just ignore them and then when I go home it does hurt. You should go out in public more, Don't worry if people laugh and stare at you, because one day they will get laughed at. When I was younger my mom bought me horses so I'd have a responsibility, and they help me like Izzy helps you

PROCLAMATION

WHEREAS, the foundation of a humane and just society is the people's willingness to work together for the common good; and

WHEREAS, children grow to be our future, and we must encourage them to become strong, productive, and caring people; and

WHEREAS, Gabrielle Ford has dedicated herself to the cause of educating our youth about the dangers and effects of bullying and the joys of embracing each others differences; and

WHEREAS, Gabrielle has triumphed in the face of her own personal adversity in order to share her gifts with the youth community; and

WHEREAS, countless articles and stories have been developed in order to chronicle the challenges and successes that Gabrielle has overcome and achieved, along with her dog Izzy;

NOW THEREFORE BE IT RESOLVED that I, Mayor Sue Osborn, along with the Fenton City Council, the citizens of the City of Fenton, and all those who have been faced with adversity in their lives, will remain grateful to Gabrielle Ford, for demonstrating strength, compassion, tolerance, and understanding through teaching the youth to build a more empathetic society.

Mayor Sue Osborn
November 21, 2008

APPENDIX

Photos

Losing Balance

Gabe at the Peltonen School of Dance

*With Mimma (left)
and Caitlin (above)*

Ready for the STAGE!

Shattered Dreams

Bullied

The hallway is where bullying often takes place.

*Suffering
in silence . . .*

*My senior sports photo. Yeah, I made it through
. . . free as a bird!*

Changes

A New Beginning!

Building a Mystery

On the phone with Grandma Hooker planning the arrival of my furry little girl.

Bob delivers my four-legged bundle of joy!

Sweet Dreams . . .

Longest ears in the litter!

Even my infamous hat couldn't stop the sunburn at Sea World.

Disney princesses

Who knew Goofy could be used as "adaptive equipment."

Madeline, a Southern Belle at the Boone Hall Plantation in South Carolina (used in the TV Miniseries North & South).

The Liver Shunt

*The rock that
started it all.*

Oakland Veterinary Referral Services

*Dr. Sandy Smith and
Dr. Cathy Anderson*

Let's go Izzy!

Yes, it hurts!

Barkley gave the gift of life—a blood donation.

A feisty fighter like me. She's up and about after surgery.

"Angel Izzy"

Landing on Animal Planet

Joe films Chris and me
for Animal Planet's A
Pet Story.

On our way to film at
Dr. Sandy's office.

A brief visit and photo
opportunity with the
wonderful Dr. Riggs,
Izzy's surgeon.

Grandma Hooker and
Izzy having a heart to
heart conversation.

*Doug Hostetter
(cameraman and
resident goofball)*

*Grandma Hooker
and Madeline*

*Izzy stylin' her
Animal Planet
bandana*

*Dan Houle, you are one in
a million. We appreciate
your friendship and support
through this journey.*

Not in My Wildest Dreams

Beecher High

Linden Elementary

My first school visits

Barhite Elementary

Above: Speaking at Scottsburg Elementary (Indiana). Photo to the right is with Izzy and my three cousins who attended Scottsburg at the time. Left: Gabe and Uncle Clayton

Above: Roswell, New Mexico

*Izabel's first portrait
- by Caitlin (my sister)*

Say Hello to Izzy!

*Northwest Airlines Staff,
you're the BEST!*
~
*Southwest Airlines,
we love you too!*

New York Ladies Trip

Ready to hit the road!

Visiting Uncle Bob and Aunt Linda in New York.

Mr. Ferris's apartment.

There were yellow cabs EVERYWHERE!

The Plaza is awesome!

Stopped for a bite at Carl's, a hamburger joint near Ground Zero.

Can't go to NYC
and not visit Times
Square!

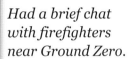

Had a brief chat
with firefighters
near Ground Zero.

Izzy taking Uncle Bob
for a walk.

Caitlin in the Versace store;
what an experience!

Two of a Kind

Madeline and Izzy off to the 4th of July parade.

Bonding time for Rick and Izzy while waiting for the parade.

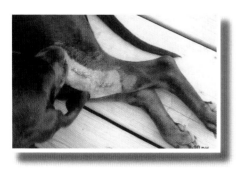

Izzy's battle scars after muscle and nerve tissue removed.

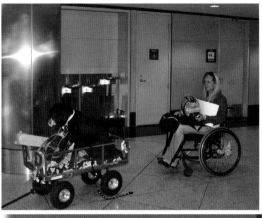

Two of a kind!

On the set of People & Pets: Common Diseases.

Sean & Samji hanging out in Southern California.

*Sean's looking for a good deal on **clementines** at the Farmer's Market in Santa Barbara.*

Winds of Adversity

Pitiful I know, but don't feel sorry
for me. I did it my way. I wasn't
going down until I was taken down.

Oh, I am in my favorite
Dominator shirt! This is the
one they cut off me when
I broke by arm.

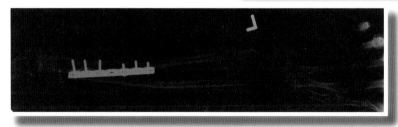

A plate, six screws—Ouch!
Oh, and it makes air travel so much fun—Not!

We "Paws" for a Thank You!

Erica and Dale Johnson,
CEO Dominator Clothing, with
Gabe and Izzy.

*Stylin' my new
Dominator jacket.*

Dale, Dominik Hasek,
and Gabe

Dominik Hasek says,
"There's a Dominator in all of us!"

A Dominator's Spirit

*Being a voice in demand means travel
and lots of it for Gabe and Izzy!*

*Below: The dynamic duo catch a few ZZZ's during an eight hour
airport layover.*

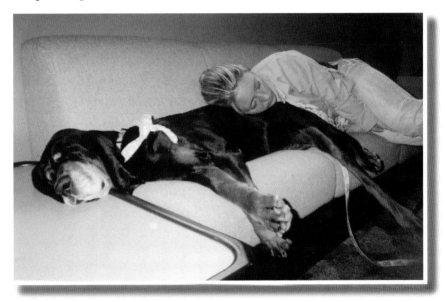

*"Hello everyone, my name is Gabrielle Ford, and this is my
best friend Iz ... zy zzzZZZzzzZZZzzzzz ...."*

It's My Party and I'll Bark If I Want To!

A Birthday Bash for Izzy

You are invited to......

Izabel's 8th Birthday Party!!!

*It's My Party and I'll **Scarf** If I Want To!*

The Year of the Rainbow

Photo by Kevin McClure

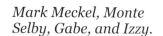
Mark Meckel, Monte Selby, Gabe, and Izzy.

Izzy wearing her AKC Honorable Mention ACE Award.

Gabe is presented with the Community Hero Award from the Fenton Chamber of Commerce.

Nathan Meckel sings "Hold On" to Gabe at the IRA Conference.

Gabe and Donna working hard? or hardly working?

Family Photos

191

To order additional copies of *Still Dancing*, or to find out about other books by Gabrielle Ford, please visit www.gabeandizzy.com.

Gabe and Izzy's anti-bullying children's storybook series coming soon!

Quantity discounts and bulk orders of *Still Dancing* are available by contacting www.gabeandizzy.com or by calling (810) 433–5667.

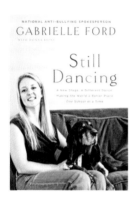

Gabe and Izzy Publishing
P.O. Box 1003
Fenton, MI 48430
(810) 433–5667

"NO SCHOOL BULLYING!"
Gabe and Izzy Publishing

Gabe, Ben and Izzy (pink scarf), Shrive Elementary, Rockwell, NC.